SUNFLOWERS

Reaktion's Botanical series is the first of its kind, integrating horticultural and botanical writing with a broader account of the cultural and social impact of trees, plants and flowers.

Sunflowers

✿

Stephen A. Harris

REAKTION BOOKS

Published by
REAKTION BOOKS LTD
Unit 32, Waterside
44–48 Wharf Road
London N1 7UX, UK

www.reaktionbooks.co.uk

First published 2018

Printed and bound in China

A catalogue record for this book is available from the British Library

ISBN 978 1 78023 926 2

Contents

❀

Annual sunflower inflorescence.

one

Amazing

❊

This flower has to all Kansans a historic symbolism which speaks of frontier days, winding trails, pathless prairies, and is full of the life and glory of the past, the pride of the present, and richly emblematic of the majesty of a golden future, and is a flower which has given Kansas the worldwide name, 'The Sunflower State'.

Session Laws of Kansas, 1 JUNE 1903[1]

In 1597 the English herbalist John Gerard appeared disappointed that the common sunflowers he grew in his garden in Holborn, London, were only 4.3 m (14 ft) tall; those of his European competitors reached a scarcely believable 7.3 m (24 ft).[2] Sunflowers, with their massive yellow flower heads surmounting a single stem and the ability of the young heads to track the sun, have attracted attention since they were introduced to Europe from the Americas in the early sixteenth century. Today they are among the most recognizable plants on Earth. Images of sunflowers are incorporated into all manner of designs, from stamps and company logos to ceramics and glassware. Briefly, in 1987, one of the canvases from Vincent van Gogh's *Sunflower* series became the most expensive painting ever sold at auction.[3] Tens of millions of hectares of land on the planet are farmed for sunflowers, and hundreds of millions of pounds are spent promoting sunflower seeds and oil as healthy foods. In July 2014 a commercial airliner en route from Amsterdam to Kuala Lumpur was shot down above Ukraine. One image of the ensuing carnage, which fleetingly held news headlines worldwide, was of pieces of wreckage peppering fields ablaze with the golden-yellow heads of ripening sunflowers.[4]

The sunflower belongs to a genus (*Helianthus*) of about fifty species from the Americas. The name 'sunflower' is merely a modern translation of an older Latin name, *flos solis*, a reference to the large flower head, while the genus name is the Greek form of this name rendered in botanical Latin. Sunflowers are part of a much larger group of plants, the sunflower family (Asteraceae), all of which are readily separated from all other flowering plants by the structure of their flower heads. The Asteraceae has been recognized as a distinct group since classical times, and is sometimes referred to as Compositae, 'composites' or even just 'comps'.

Other than sunflowers, the sunflower family is most familiar to us as daisies, dandelions and thistles, but also includes lettuces, artichokes and arnica. Few British lawns will be without collections of daisies, with their spoon-shaped leaves, or dandelions, with their toothed, spear-shaped leaves. Solitary dandelions and clumps of daisies are perennials, resistant to the mechanical grazing of lawn-mowers; the beauty each yellow or white flower head adds to a lawn tarnishes the soul of those gardeners who strive to exert absolute control over nature.

The Asteraceae is the world's largest family of flowering plants, containing approximately 32,000 species; on average, nine in every hundred flowering plant species you find on the planet will be members. Naturally, members of the family occur in almost all habitats, from the Arctic to the Antarctic. They are found from the driest deserts of Arabia and South Africa to the high mountains of the Andes and Himalayas, from the swamps of North America to the grasslands of central Asia and from polar tundra to urban wastelands. Most Asteraceae are herbs, but in the tropics and on oceanic islands they become shrubs and trees.

Despite being well defined as a family, the identification of individual Asteraceae species is often difficult. In Europe and North

Chrysanthemum Indicum annuum
maximum, sive flos solis major.

Great annual Sunflower.

Herb. Bobart

A mid-17th-century specimen of common sunflower from Jacob Bobart the Younger's herbarium. This was probably grown in the Oxford Physic Garden.

America, many Asteraceae are yellow. However, in the tropics, Asteraceae with purple, lilac, red or white flowers are familiar. At first sight, some highly adapted species, such as the giant groundsels of Mount Kilimanjaro in Kenya, the hedgehog thistles of Arabian deserts, or alpine edelweiss, do not even look like Asteraceae.

Dandelions are commonly found in artificial habitats and disturbed areas throughout the temperate regions of the world.

Given the size of the family, one might expect it to have great economic value. However, compared to other plant families – such as the grasses, beans and roses – few Asteraceae are used as food or medicine. Yet thousands of different insects and hundreds of vertebrates need Asteraceae and the habitats they create. In current environmental jargon, the Asteraceae are major providers of environmental services, such as food sources for crop pollinators, including bees and hoverflies. The Asteraceae are essential components of many ornamental gardens, and an ornamental zinnia was probably the first plant to flower in space.[5]

This book explores the biology, ecology and cultural significance of the sunflower family, and in this first chapter we follow the lifecycle of the sunflower to illustrate the basic structure of the family. The next chapter shows how morphological variation on the sunflower theme produces the enormous global diversity shown by the family. Morphological, anatomical, physiological and biochemical adaptations of the Asteraceae make them botanical survivors. Chapter Three shows how the Asteraceae survive, adapt and evolve across environments. Chapters Four and Five focus on the abilities of the family to cure, kill or feed us. Chapter Six describes how the sunflower was transformed from a minor Native American food plant into a global commodity. The final three chapters are concerned with the symbolism of Asteraceae, their role as inspiration for art and literature, and how they have come to fill our gardens with some of our most commonly cultivated plants. Moreover, images of Asteraceae have been used by advertisers to peddle influence and market all manner of things from lifestyles to sanitary and health products, and to boost environmental aspiration.

Hans Hoffmann, *A Hare in the Forest*, c. 1585, showing a hare surrounded by a ground flora of thistle, bellflower, ladies mantle and dock.

Germination

For many children, the common sunflower is the first – and some-times only – experience they get of the potential locked away in a seed. When planted in damp soil, a dry, grey-and-black-striped 'seed', familiar as rabbit or parrot food and scarcely 1 cm ($^1\!/_3$ in.) long, will grow within a few months into a plant several metres tall, topped by a huge yellow flower. Gerard wrote with wonder of the transformation:

> a plant of such stature and talenesse, that in one sommer being sowen of a seede in Aprill, it hath risen up to the height of fourteene foote [4.3 m] in my garden, where one flower was in waight three pounde and two ounces [1.4 kg], and crosse ouerthwart the flower a measure sixteene inches [40 cm] broade.[6]

Break open a sunflower 'seed' and inside is a grey-brown, elliptical kernel covered in a fine membrane; the kernel is the true seed and the membrane the seed coat. The kernel splits into a pair of large, flat, rectangular, oil-rich structures (cotyledons or seed leaves) and, between them, a tiny embryo that eventually forms the new plant.

Within days of planting the 'seed', germination starts below ground level. A primary root emerges from the embryo to anchor the seedling in the soil. The germinating seed starts to absorb water, and the first shoot emerges as the cotyledons expand. The stem imme-diately below the cotyledons grows and forms a hook as the shoot forces its way towards the surface of the soil. At the surface, the hook straightens, pulling the cotyledons and shoot tip away from the soil into the air. The energy to get this far has come from the oils in the cotyledons, but they have one final job to do: they become the seed-ling's first leaves. The cotyledons turn green and start to photosyn-thesize, converting water and carbon dioxide into sugar and oxygen

A bumblebee visiting knapweed.

using chlorophyll and the power of sunlight. Within a week of first greening the cotyledons wither as true leaves, produced by the rapidly developing shoot, take over the process of photosynthesis.

Seed germination is a fascinating process to observe. The ready availability of time-lapse photography enables a process that takes days to be replayed in minutes. It has transformed our view of germination and more generally of plants as stationary organisms.[7] As the full beauty of sunflower germination is replayed, seedlings are seen to

In the 17th century, sunflowers were cultivated novelties known for their size and the movement of their flower heads.

British earthenware dish with sunflower decoration made by F. Gadesden in 1876.

sway gently, while the cotyledons and new leaves flap languidly. The growth movements of plants were among the events captured by the German botanist Wilhelm Pfeffer at the end of the nineteenth century, in the pioneering days of time-lapse photography.[8] A few years earlier Charles Darwin had painstakingly plotted the movements of hundreds of plant species on sheets of glass and reported his observations in his final work, *The Power of Movement in Plants* (1880). He coined the term 'circumnutation' for the phenomenon, reporting that its extent and speed vary among species; sunflower seedlings moved about 3 mm ($^1/_{10}$ in.) every fourteen hours.[9] Darwin could not explain circumnutation, but concluded that it was fundamental to a 'plant's physiology'.

In 1967 Anders Johnsson and Donald Israelsson proposed the idea of gravity-powered circumnutation.[10] However, Johnsson had to wait nearly forty years before he could take advantage of the facilities on board the International Space Station, to test the hypothesis. Sunflower 'seeds' and seedlings are too large for the confined conditions of space flight, so instead the tiny seeds of a model plant species, thale cress, were used.[11] Seeds were germinated in a special chamber for studying the long-term effects of gravity and the seedlings photographed to monitor their exact positions. In the near weightlessness of the space station, minute circumnutation was observed. Darwin was right: the phenomenon was hardwired but gravity amplified the effect.[12] Extraterrestrial experimentation had answered a fundamental biological question literally rooted in earth.

Flowering and Fruiting

Back on Earth, a sunflower seedling must grow rapidly if it is to complete its lifecycle during the short northern temperate summers. As the stem lengthens, rough, spirally arranged, heart-shaped leaves are added. The sunflower stem, a rigid, pith-packed cylinder, must be strong to support the flower head (capitulum), which can be up to 60 cm (24 in.) in diameter. Despite appearances, the capitulum is not a single flower; it is a collection of thousands of tiny flowers surrounded by rows of green, leaf-like structures called involucral bracts. Look carefully at a sunflower head and you will see two types of flower (floret). Around the outside of the head are sterile, bilaterally symmetrical ray florets with large, yellow, strap-like petals. Inside the ray florets, whose function is to attract pollinators, are hundreds of fertile tube florets with symmetrical, brown petals, 'set as though a cunning workman had of purpose placed them in very good order'.[13] The mathematical regularity of the interlocking curves produced by the tube florets has spawned spurious mystical interpretations. More prosaically, the pattern is a natural consequence of packing the maximum number of objects into a minimal area (see Chapter Eight).

Examine the tube floret; it has all the elements of a typical flower (calyx, corolla, stamens, carpels), albeit highly modified. The calyx (pappus) is reduced to two bristles, while the corolla comprises five fused petals. Inside the corolla are five stamens, each of which

Close-up of annual sunflower head showing disc florets.

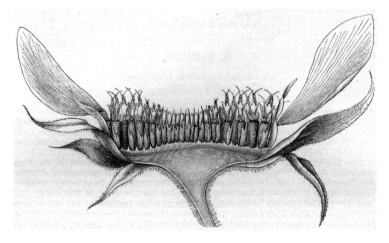

Vertical section through a sunflower head showing its structure and the different sorts of florets.

comprises a bag of pollen (anther) on a stalk (filament). The stamens are joined into a ring by their anthers, while the filaments are attached to the corolla. At the centre of the flower is a needle-like style. Pollen is deposited inside the anther ring and forced out of the top as the style grows, rather like a plunger forcing liquid out of a syringe. Once above the pollen plug, the tip of the style splits and curls back to reveal the receptive, stigmatic surface ready to receive male pollen. Beneath the corolla and pappus is the ovary, which is attached to the receptacle of the flower head and is associated with a small flap of tissue.

The stages of pollen release can be seen by observing tube florets from the outside towards the inside of the flower head. Tube florets closest to the outside have curled-back-style lobes with a few scattered pollen grains on their surface; a little further inside, the style of the tube florets has yet to divide. Further in still, there is a plug of yellow pollen on top of each newly opened tube floret, while towards the centre of the flower head, the tube florets have yet to open. The highly visible flower head means insect pollinators, including specialist and generalist bees and hoverflies, are readily attracted to sunflowers.[14] For their services in promoting the spatial movement of genes between individual plants, pollinators are rewarded with a pollen meal.

Once pollinated and fertilized, each tube floret produces one single-seeded, dry fruit, technically called a cypsela, which does not break open to release the seed. In common with most people's use, this book will refer to Asteraceae 'fruits' as 'seeds', unless made otherwise clear. In its native North American range, the oil-rich seeds of wild sunflowers are consumed by small birds and mammals, although their precise role in dispersing the seeds has been questioned. An alternative natural disperser of sunflower seeds may be bison; their dense fur may trap seeds which eventually become dislodged as the animal moves.[15] Seeds of the common sunflower can remain viable, as part of seed banks, for at least four years.[16] Consequently, genes inside sunflower seeds move in space based on how far animals transport them, and in time based on how long they remain part of the seed bank.

The cycle of germination, growth, flowering and seed production, common to all Asteraceae, will vary depending on which of the many thousands of different Asteraceae species is being investigated. Asteraceae variation is the subject of the next chapter.

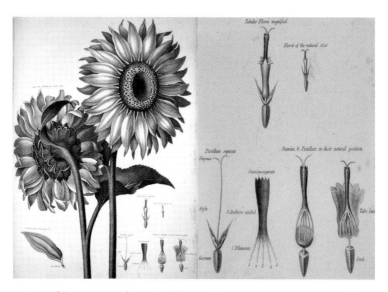

Parts of the Asteraceae flower head illustrated by a 19th-century engraving of the common sunflower that was designed as a teaching aid.

Favourite garden sunflowers and daisies from John Parkinson's *Paradisus Terrestris* (1629): (i) 'corne marigold of Candy'; (ii) 'flower of the sunne'; (iii) 'marigold'; (iv) 'purple marigold'; (v) 'golden mouse-eare'; (vi) 'Spanish vipers grasse'; (vii) 'goe to bed at noon'.

two

Varying

❖

With all the wealth of our gardens there are many curious types of vegetation still quite under represented . . . the majority of these forms of life are more curious than beautiful but . . . they often afford more pleasure and information than the more showy members of the vegetable kingdom.

W. H. BAXTER, *The Garden* (1877)[1]

During 1812, a year before he became head gardener at the Oxford Physic Garden (now the Botanic Garden), William Baxter recorded more than five hundred plant species around the city; over sixty were members of the sunflower family.[2] In February and March he recorded coltsfoot and butterbur, which flower before they produce leaves; also in flower were common daisy and groundsel. By May the walls of the colleges were graced with Oxford ragwort, a plant then all but unique to the city. June and July produced many white-, yellow-, blue- and purple-flowered Asteraceae, for example bristly oxtongue, burdock, chicory, common ragwort, cudweeds, feverfew, hawkbit, knapweeds, mugwort, oxeye daisy, sowthistles, thistles and yarrows. In the late summer and early autumn these gave way to carline thistles, bur- and corn marigolds, hawkweeds, tansy, wild lettuce and wormwood. However, the diversity of Asteraceae around nineteenth-century Oxford, although representative of that in Britain, is a mere fraction of the family's global diversity.

Eighteenth- and nineteenth-century expeditions across the globe returned to Europe loaded with specimens of Asteraceae, often very different from those native to Europe. Variations on the sunflower theme appeared infinite; the Almighty's beetle fixation was matched by a fondness for Asteraceae. We can estimate that there are more than 32,000 species of Asteraceae because plant taxonomists, those scientists who discover, describe and classify plant variation, have been cataloguing the diversity of the world's plants for more than five centuries. Taxonomists frequently belie their caricature as rather eccentric creatures who spend most of their time sifting dusty, dried specimens. Attention to detail, a good botanical eye and luck are certainly necessary, but a successful taxonomist must also get out into the world's wild places. We have no idea what plants might inhabit such places, let alone what numbers of Asteraceae they might contain. Although wild places still exist, they are under great threat: approximately 10 per cent of their total area was lost in two decades between the early 1990s and mid-2010s.[3]

The distinctive Asteraceae flower head, first described in sixteenth-century France by Jean Ruel, has been used to group thistle- and daisy-like plants since at least 300 BC.[4] Our understanding of Asteraceae variation blossomed during the eighteenth and nineteenth centuries through the work of a handful of European and American synantherologists (scientists who study Asteraceae).[5] Despite their great capacity for hard work, early synantherologists, the architects of modern Asteraceae classification, could have made their advances only through the efforts of hundreds of frequently overlooked botanical navvies, who collected and collated the specimens that fill the world's great botanical museums and herbaria.

Worldwide, there are approximately 2,500 herbaria containing about 300 million herbarium specimens (dried plants). In the Muséum National d'Histoire Naturelle in Paris, for example, there are around 10 million specimens; the New York Botanical Garden has about 8 million, and the Royal Botanic Gardens Kew about 7 million.[6] Enormous investment has been made in these scientific collections since the Renaissance, partially because they are thought of as the gold standard for recording the plants around us – the resources upon which our lives depend – and because we are curious about life on Earth. Since 1970 the number of specimens in the world's herbaria has doubled, and one estimate suggests that as many as half the world's undescribed flowering plant species have already been collected.[7] More sobering still is the estimate that over half of the world's specimens are wrongly named.[8] Yet neither of these observations should detract from the central role herbaria play in understanding patterns

Gnaphalium coarctatum, a widespread American member of the Asteraceae.

Scaly blazing star cultivated in the garden of Eltham Palace in 1726, as illustrated by Johann Dillenius in the *Hortus Elthamensis* (1732) and the associated herbarium specimen.

of Asteraceae variation; scientific collections are an international, intergenerational compact of trust among collectors, curators and institutions.

Discovering Variation

The discovery of a new flowering plant is a frequent phenomenon; about 2,000 new plants are described annually. New species are not only discovered in remote places but may be found close to major cities. Furthermore, they are not necessarily diminutive; they may be highly visible parts of a landscape, but it may simply be that people have not taken the time to collect them and find out whether they are new. The journeys made by plant collectors in search of new species have transformed our understanding of the natural world beyond utilitarian justifications for being interested in plants. In the British Isles, the seventeenth-century naturalist John Ray of Essex broke with the traditional focus on plants as medicine or food; he was interested in plants for what they told us about how the natural world worked.[9] Ray travelled around Britain and Europe cataloguing the plants he saw, as he tried to make sense of them. One of his earliest works was an account of the plants of Cambridgeshire, a so-called Flora. Ray's *Catalogus plantarum circa Cantabrigiam nascentium* (1660) is the first County Flora in Britain; today there are hundreds of such Floras.[10]

On the Continent, freed from the encumbrance of religious study by the death of his father, the 22-year-old Frenchman Joseph Pitton de Tournefort spent the last thirty years of his life studying and collecting plants.[11] As a collector he was adventurous; on one occasion in the Pyrenees

he found in these vast solitudes a subsistence similar to one of the most austere Anchorites, and the unfortunate inhabitants provided him with what they were able; not many others than he had thieves to fear. Also it [the Pyrenees] was repeatedly plundered by Spanish Miquelets [mountain troops] and [they] imagined a stratagem to steal some money on these kinds of occasions. He put the Réaux [coins] in bread that he carried on him, and that was so black and so hard, that although the thieves were strong and scorned not people who had nothing, they treated him with contempt.[12]

Between 1700 and 1702 Tournefort ventured into the eastern Mediterranean, accompanied by the French artist Claude Aubriet and the German botanist Andreas von Gundelsheimer, to record the plants of the Ottoman Empire.[13] Tournefort collected hundreds of plant specimens, which were deposited in herbaria in Paris, London and Oxford; among those specimens were many Asteraceae. He discussed the specimens in his published books, including *Relation d'un voyage du Levant* (1717).

Tournefort's expedition inspired the Oxford professor John Sibthorp and one of the world's finest botanical artists, Ferdinand Bauer, to explore the region more than eighty years later. Sibthorp's expedition secured over 2,400 herbarium specimens, while Bauer made pencil sketches that were later transformed into nearly 1,000 watercolours. The watercolours were eventually published in the *Flora Graeca* (1806–40), one of the most expensive botanical books ever written, and now extremely rare. Among the watercolours are 149 images of Asteraceae, dozens of which were new to science.

The arid regions of temperate South Africa proved rich Asteraceae-collecting grounds for botanical explorers such as the Englishman William Burchell and the German Johann Franz Drège. South African species such as the African daisy, the rain daisy and the king-fisher daisy could not only fill herbarium cabinets, they could be readily grown in European gardens. Plants in cultivation could be studied alive, revealing aspects of their biology that were impossible to investigate in herbarium specimens, such as their reproductive biology and physiology.

During the nineteenth century vast numbers of new species of Asteraceae were discovered at high altitudes in the Andes of South

Asteraceae species and their distributions are discovered through exploration. These four species were collected as part of an expedition to the eastern Mediterranean, the results of which were eventually published as the *Flora Graeca* (1806–40): *Carduncellus caeruleus*; *Echinops microcephalus*; *Achillea holosericea*; *Staehelina petiolata* (clockwise from top left).

Cerrado vegetation, a vast Asteraceae-rich habitat in central Brazil.

America, but, although Amazonia was a honey pot for plant exploration, there were few Asteraceae compared to montane and arid regions. Between 1836 and 1841 the young Scottish surgeon George Gardner travelled thousands of kilometres through the Brazilian interior on foot and by horse to explore regions that were unknown to most Europeans.[14] He explored the evergreen, mist-covered *mata atlântica* forests in the southeast, the vastness of the *cerrado* in the centre of the country and the inhospitable *caatinga* of the northeast. As he travelled he collected more than 9,000 plant specimens; about 13 per cent of his collection was Asteraceae specimens, of which more than half were new species.[15]

For Gardner, the major limitation to the acquisition of specimens was the ability to travel and transport them safely. Today global travel and transport are not nearly so difficult, although problems with personal safety remain. A major concern for the modern plant collector is obtaining permission to collect and study legally and ethically. Plant collecting is an important cultural activity, but some people argue that such activities damage the cultures of indigenous peoples and settlers. Plant collectors are sometimes compared to modern-day Hercules stealing the golden apples of the Hesperides, while foreign collectors are said to encourage local people to give away their traditional knowledge for no return.[16] Attempts to deal with such problems have been made through adopting ethical approaches to collecting, abiding by the terms of international agreements such as the Nagoya Protocol and cultivating extensive local networks of personal relationships.[17] Today plant collectors cannot, and should not be able to, operate without the informed consent of the countries in which they work.

Networks of botanical communication, essential for the circulation and testing of ideas, are forged by shared fieldwork and personal visits, and by the exchange of specimens and letters.[18] An example of the complexities of such networks, and the ambiguity of names, relates to the introduction of the hybrid plant Oxford ragwort to Britain from Sicily.[19] Evidence for the introduction of this plant to the Oxford Physic Garden comes from herbarium and literature records. Specimen-based evidence suggests that ragwort seeds were given to the botanist and diplomat William Sherard by the priest and naturalist Francesco Cupani of Sicily in the early eighteenth century. Sherard, who was tutor to the grandson of the Dowager Duchess of Beaufort at Badminton, Mary Somerset, passed the seeds on to his employer. The duchess, one of the foremost gardeners and naturalists of her day, had an extensive network of contacts across Britain and Europe, including the head of the Oxford Botanic Garden, Jacob Bobart the Younger. From Bobart's time until the early nineteenth century, Oxford ragwort was a novelty confined to the city's walls and a few parishes looked after by Oxford-trained prelates who wanted to remember their student days. Today it is found in much of Britain. Piecing together the story of the botanical relationships among these people is possible only from physical plant specimens, since Oxford ragwort is readily confused with other European ragworts.

Naming Variation

Peoples across the world have always invented names for the plants and animals they have discovered. Yet taxonomists are sometimes disparagingly described as 'stamp collectors'. Such ignorant criticism fails to recognize that giving a name to an organism is an essential first step in starting to understand its biology. Names are a way of organizing information and ought to facilitate communication among cultures and across generations. The important thing about a name is that it refers unambiguously to something. Common, vernacular or trivial names are used in everyday life to refer to plants and animals, but these same organisms also have scientific or Latin names. All known Asteraceae species have scientific names; few have common names. Common names enjoy neither uniformity nor international recognition; instead they reflect people's cultures, traditions, beliefs and prejudices.[20]

A scientific name aims at stability, is applied unambiguously and is understood across language barriers. The sunflower, *Helianthus annuus*, was formally described by the Swedish naturalist Carolus Linnaeus in his *Species Plantarum* (1753). Before Linnaeus the plant sported phrase names such as 'Herba maxima', given by Rembert Dodoens in his *Pemptades* (1616), or 'Helenium indicum maximum', used by Gaspard Bauhin in his *Pinax theatri botanici* (1623). Linnaeus' innovation was the consistent application of a simple binomial naming system, which today is governed by *The International Code of Botanical Nomenclature* (2011). The first name, *Helianthus* ('flower of the sun'), is the genus name and refers to a group of more than fifty species. The second word, *annuus* ('annual'), uniquely identifies a particular species. Below the level of the species there may also be subspecies, varieties and forms. According to the *Code*, once a name has been published formally, inadvertent mistakes cannot be changed. The genus *Scalesia* is found only in the Galapagos archipelago and is among the relatives of the true sunflowers.[21] In 1836 the genus was named by the Scottish botanist George Walker-Arnott in honour of 'W. Scales'. Unfortunately, Walker-Arnott made a mistake: Scales did not exist, and the gentleman he meant to commemorate was William Stables.[22] Rather than honouring a botanist, *Scalesia* commemorates an orthographic error.

SENECIO SQUALIDUS. *INELEGANT RAGWORT.*

Oxford ragwort, a species introduced to Oxford from Sicily but now common across the British Isles.

Every scientific name must be associated with a particular specimen (type), permanently preserved in a scientific collection. The type is the specimen an author used when creating the name. For example, in the case of *Helianthus annuus* the type is in Linnaeus' personal herbarium, which is today owned by the Linnean Society of London. The type does not have to be typical of a specific species; it is the taxonomist's job to discover where variation in one species ends and another begins. Despite the *Code*, some species have numerous scientific names (synonyms), in addition to the accepted name, because of the discovery of earlier valid names or new research. Such discoveries may necessitate a change of scientific name. Despite the importance of scientific names, common names will be used in this book, where possible; a complete list of scientific equivalents is given in the Appendix.

Flower Heads, Florets and Fruits

Asteraceae are usually annual or perennial herbs (such as the common sunflower or the European cornflower), and some are shrubs or trees (such as the New Zealand daisy bush, the African camphor bush or the Central American *tubú*). Very few are climbers or epiphytes (among them Brazilian *guaco*, Central American *Gongrostylus*), aquatics (such as the Mexican oak leaf plant) or succulents (such as the Canarian *verode*).

Many Asteraceae, like those found by Baxter, have yellow flower heads and appear superficially similar, giving rise to the acronym NYC (Nasty Yellow Composite) among some who try to identify them. Describing Asteraceae species requires close attention to details of the flower head, other than just colour, including the types, arrangement and gender of the florets.[23] In homogamous ('same marriage') flower heads all florets are bisexual (with male and female parts); very rarely are all florets in a flower head male or female. Bisexual, homogamous flower heads are found in lettuce and dandelion, whereas male and female, unisexual flower heads may be found on the same plant (as in cocklebur) or different plants (as in baccharis). In contrast, heterogamous ('different marriage') flower heads are like those of the sunflower: the florets are a mixture of bisexual inner florets and female or sterile outer florets. The involucral bracts surrounding the florets may occur in one or more rows. Bracts may be leaf- or scale-like, hairy, bristly, succulent or elaborately ornamented, even spiny. The receptacle, on which the florets sit in the capitulum, is usually flat but may be

African thistle, *Berkheya multijuga*.

conical or cylindrical (as in the toothache plant and coneflowers), and occasionally it is adorned with scales, bristles or hairs.

The number of florets per flower head ranges from one in the globe thistles to more than 1,000 in the true sunflowers. The sunflower flower head has two types of floret: those with radially symmetrical corollas and those with bilaterally symmetrical corollas. Across the whole family there are four types of bilaterally symmetrical floret, but the most frequent are ray florets, which usually have three-toothed corollas (as in camomile), or ligulate florets, which usually have five-toothed corollas (as in hawkweed). One way to imagine the flower head is as a flowering spike that has been squashed vertically; the florets on the edge of the flower head correspond to the flowers at the base of the spike, and the florets at the centre of the flower head to those at the tip of the spike. Flower heads themselves may be aggregated into even more complex structures, and sometimes those structures are surrounded by more bracts. The arrangement and number of flower heads, their size and their shape vary across species and genera. Common flower-head arrangements include the solitary ones of the common daisy and the flat-headed arrangement of common ragwort; less common are the spikes of blazing stars.

Other important features across the Asteraceae are the pollen-containing anthers and the structures (styles) upon which pollen grains land. Anthers vary dramatically in shape and/or size, including extensions to their bases and the appendages at their tips. Typically, styles have two arms, each with a receptive stigmatic surface. The style and its arms may be hairy, covered with rounded protuberances or hairless, and there may also be appendages on the arms. Stigmatic surfaces may be arranged along the margin or on the entire inner surfaces of the style arms.

Asteraceae fruits are typically dry and do not break apart at maturity but have a pappus, the remnants of the calyx; in the sunflower, the pappus drops off once the fruit is mature. Fruits can be angular,

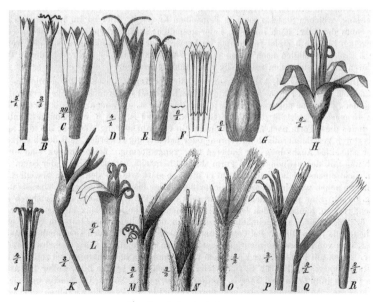

Floret variation in Asteraceae.

Inflorescence of yarrow cultivar.

rounded, compressed, curved, elaborately ornamented or winged, their surfaces hairless, hairy or even glandular. Very rarely, fruits are fleshy, as in the invasive South African bitou bush, where the mature fruits are arranged like beads around the edge of the flower head. The pappus aids fruit dispersal, and is familiar to generations of children as a makeshift timepiece, the dandelion clock. Each elongated fruit in the pompom is topped by a single ring of fine hairs. Across the family, the pappus varies in structure from being made of smooth, barbed or plumed hairs through scales to flexible or stiff bristles, in single or multiple rows.

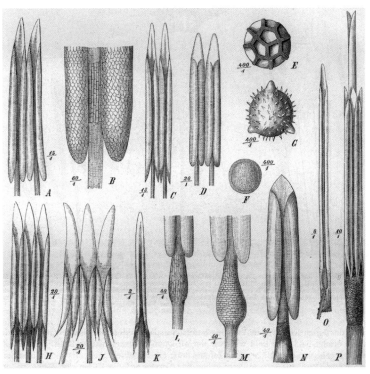

Anther variation in Asteraceae.

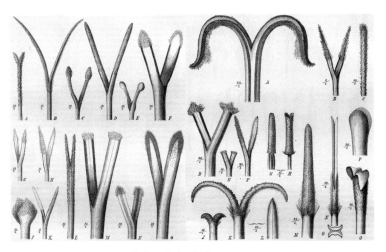

Style variation in Asteraceae.

Arranging the Pieces

The Asteraceae belong to a large group of the flowering plants called eudicots, which includes the majority of familiar plants such as roses, legumes (for example peas, beans and clovers), carnations, cabbages and oaks. About 10 per cent of the 290,000 eudicot species belong to the order Asterales, which, in addition to the sunflowers, includes the bellflowers, bogbeans and goodenias.[24] Within the Asterales, the closest living relatives of the sunflower family are found in a small family of South American herbs, called the Calyceraceae, about which we know little.

The first early modern attempts to arrange the variation found in the Asteraceae were those of Tournefort,[25] whose academic reputation was based on the *Institutiones Rei Herbariae* (1700) and his active hostility to the evidence that plants reproduced sexually.[26] Plant sexuality, demonstrated by Rudolf Camerarius in *De sexu plantarum epistola* (1694), was advocated strongly by Tournefort's pupil Sébastien Vaillant, much to the master's displeasure. Vaillant, a musician, surgeon and eventually botanist, was employed as a popular Demonstrator at the Jardin du Roi, Paris. Tournefort recognized that the flower head was composed of numerous florets, sometimes of different types, and divided the Asteraceae into three broad groups: those with discoid flower heads, ligulate flower heads and radiate flower heads. Given Vaillant's interests in plant sexuality, it is unsurprising that his own ordering of the Asteraceae stressed floret gender, although he also divided the Asteraceae into three broad groups: thistles; chicories and lettuces; and the rest of the Asteraceae. In the mid-eighteenth century Linnaeus did little with the sunflowers and their relatives other than place them into one (the Syngenesia) of the 24 classes of his Sexual Classification System.

The man who changed our understanding of the Asteraceae was another Frenchman, the early nineteenth-century lawyer and jurist Henri de Cassini. Unlike Tournefort and Vaillant, the squeamish Cassini confined his interests in the natural world to his spare time,

Fruit and flowers of the common dandelion during a British spring.

claiming: 'I focused my entire attention on the living but insensitive beings [plants] that were so abundant around me, very variable and graceful, and that I could mutilate, dissect and destroy without inspiring pity in me.'[27] During 22 years of systematic, painstaking, microscopic investigation of Asteraceae styles, anthers, corollas and fruits, Cassini extracted order from what had previously been regarded as chaos; he believed he had produced a natural system of classification, as opposed to the artificial systems of previous researchers. Yet the rough-and-tumble of academic life disillusioned him as colleagues questioned his results, derided his conclusions and became jealous of his reputation; he died of cholera when he was 51 years old. Cassini's arrangement of the Asteraceae is the backbone of our current classification. His conclusions, based on enlightened, detailed observations using little more than a microscope, have been confirmed by all manner of modern approaches, including chemistry, electron microscopy and DNA sequence analyses. Cassini even correctly placed the family Calyceraceae as one of the closest relatives of the Asteraceae.

The nineteenth-century German botanist Christian Lessing's brilliant career as a synantherologist was over by the time he was 25 years old; he developed business interests in Siberia which eventually failed, ruining him financially. Among his contributions during his brief, glorious foray into the study of Asteraceae was the production of the first botanical keys that helped to identify species in the

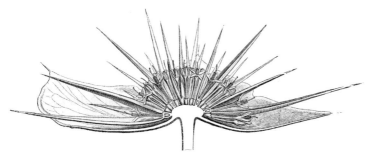

Vertical section through the inflorescence of *Calycera eryngioides*, a member of the family most closely related to the Asteraceae.

Fruiting head of a species of the South American genus *Lessingianthus*, named in honour of Christian Lessing.

family. At about the same time as Lessing was working, in Bavaria the physician Carl Heinrich 'Bipontinus' Schultz was found guilty of treason and given an unlimited prison sentence. Incarcerated, Bipontinus developed an interest in Asteraceae, grew them in the prison grounds and even published his first scientific papers on the family. He was released after three years, made the appropriate apologies, 'retired' as a revolutionary and became a hospital doctor, studying Asteraceae in his spare time. By the time of his death in 1867, he had amassed one of the finest herbaria of Asteraceae in the world and published extensively on the family, particularly the chicories and lettuces.

The study of the Asteraceae was not entirely the preserve of continental Europeans. In nineteenth-century Britain, George Bentham made monumental contributions to the classification of many plant families, including the Asteraceae, and he is regarded as one of the great taxonomic botanists. In early twentieth-century North America, Benjamin Lincoln Robinson took over the Gray Herbarium at Harvard University and focused much of his research on bringing order to the complexities of the boneset tribe (Eupatorieae). The Spanish botanist José Cuatrecasas Arumí escaped from Franco's Spain after the Civil War, establishing himself first in Colombia and then in the United States. He made key contributions to our understanding of the Asteraceae of the *páramos* in the northern Andes, especially the group known as the frailejóns. In Argentina, the Spaniard Ángel Cabrera made key contributions to the classification of South American Asteraceae.

Gene Power

Within a human lifetime, breathtaking technological and intellectual revolutions have contributed directly to our understanding of how plants work, how they are related to each other and how we interact with them. High-speed computing has become cheap, while the flow of huge datasets across continents is commonplace. Advances in computing have also brought images of the entire planet to one's desktop, and global positioning devices mean that we can know the precise location of specimens collected in the field. Furthermore, we can investigate the unifying principle of modern biology, Darwinian evolution, as never before. The vista Charles Darwin, Alfred Russel Wallace and the Moravian monk Gregor Mendel opened to our understanding of the diversity of life on Earth is based on variation in natural populations, the inheritance of genetic information from one generation to the next, and the selection over time of genetic types that are adapted to particular environments.

Plant genes are strung along the double helix of the DNA molecule, which is wound into discrete structures called chromosomes. In a typical Asteraceae, the nucleus of every cell, except those of pollen and eggs, contains two sets of chromosomes (that is to say, two genomes);

such plants are described as diploid. For example, the cultivated sunflower contains 34 chromosomes, seventeen in each genome. In diploid sunflowers each gene can exist in two forms. The form of the gene that is expressed is described as dominant over the other, recessive form. If the two forms are the same, the individual is homozygous (either dominant or recessive) for that gene, and if the two forms are different the individual is heterozygous. Consider a gene that usually produces a yellow corolla but occasionally, because of a rare mutation, produces a white corolla. If there is at least one copy of the yellow form of the gene, then the plant will have yellow corollas, but if there are two copies of the white form of the gene the corollas will be white; yellow is dominant over white. The genetic constitution of a sunflower is its genotype; the expression of that genotype, in a particular environment, is its phenotype. Furthermore, as Mendel demonstrated in the latter half of the nineteenth century, the outcome of crosses between different genotypes is predictable.

Sunflowers with more than two chromosome sets are called polyploids. For example, species with four chromosome sets are tetraploids, and those with six sets are hexaploids. Polyploids with odd numbers of chromosome sets, such as triploids (those with three sets), tend to be sterile. Polyploidy is a major force in plant evolution.[28] It generally complicates the types of genetic outcomes that are possible from sexual reproduction, but it is a means of storing genetic variation away from the effects of selection in natural populations.

Data from DNA sequences has enabled us to revise our understanding of relationships among members of the Asteraceae derived from classical studies of morphology. Indeed, the potential of DNA for understanding the evolution of all flowering plants was established in the late 1980s from research on the Asteraceae. Within the structure of a piece of DNA there are clues to the evolutionary relationships among species. DNA is found in three places in a plant cell: the nucleus, chloroplasts (where photosynthesis happens) and mitochondria (the cell's powerhouse). The DNA in each location has different origins, and is therefore useful for answering different types of evolutionary questions. At its simplest, nuclear DNA is inherited from both of a plant's parents, while chloroplast and mitochondrial DNA is inherited from one parent (usually the mother). DNA may contain thousands of characters suitable for evolutionary investigation, far more than are available from morphology, anatomy or chemistry. Furthermore, DNA offers the possibility of comparing Asteraceae species that superficially appear very different. The trick is to find DNA sequences that evolve at a rate appropriate for the problem being investigated. If the sequence evolves too rapidly, ancient relationships will be erased, but if it evolves too slowly, recent relationships will be invisible.

A New Order

Today Asteraceae species are split into twelve subfamilies and 42 tribes, although the vast majority of species are found in only three of the subfamilies: Asteroideae (twenty tribes, about 1,200 genera, 16,000 species, including sunflowers and marigolds); Cichorioideae (seven tribes, about 250 genera, 2,800 species, including lettuce and sowthistles); and Carduoideae (four tribes, about eighty genera, 2,500 species, including thistles and knapweeds).[29] The general picture to emerge since the mid-1980s is that the South American subfamily Barnadesioideae (nine genera, about ninety species) is at the base of the Asteraceae tree of life. All members of the Asteraceae, except the Barnadesioideae, have a large piece of chloroplast DNA that is inverted relative to that of all other flowering plants.[30] This type of mutation is extremely rare and therefore likely only to have happened once, at the point when the rest of the Asteraceae split from the Barnadesioideae. The Barnadesioideae and five other subfamilies (with about fifty genera and about eight hundred species), which are also primarily South American, comprise the so-called basal groups. The three core subfamilies (Carduoideae, Cichorioideae and Asteroideae), together with three tiny subfamilies (of six genera and nine species), in the evolutionary tree are distributed across the geographic range of the Asteraceae. However, the precise limits of the subfamilies, and the numbers of species they contain, remain the subject of active academic dispute.

If one assumes that a particular number of mutations occurs every million years in a DNA sequence, by counting mutations between pairs of species it is possible to determine how long ago they shared a common ancestor. That is, with each tick of the molecular clock, another mutation occurs in a piece of DNA. To investigate DNA changes millions of years ago it is necessary to have sequences where the molecular clock ticks slowly and regularly. Fossils are crucial to calibrate the tick, since they can fix dates. Plant fossils include leaves, wood,

Typical appearance of six of the largest subfamilies of Asteraceae: Asteroideae (*Coreopsis basalis*); Cichorioideae (*Scorzonera undulata*); Carduoideae (*Cirsium grahamii*); Barnadesioideae (*Barnadesia caryophylla*); Mutisioideae (*Mutisia orbignyana*); Stifftioideae (*Stifftia chrysantha*) (left to right, top to bottom).

Gonospermum fruticosum, a Canary Island endemic that is closely related to the tansy genus.

flowers, fruits and pollen grains. Pollen walls contain sporopollenin, one of the most chemically inert, stable polymers on the planet, and consequently they are resistant to chemical, fungal and bacterial decomposition and can remain preserved in soils and sediments for millions of years. Moreover, the surface of pollen grains is frequently sculpted in ways that make plant families and sometimes genera readily identifiable. A spectacular fossilized Asteraceae flower head was recovered from northern Patagonian rocks that are approximately 47 million years old.[31] Even older Asteraceae pollen grains, from the subfamily Barnadesioideae, have been found buried in Antarctic sediments between 66 and 76 million years old.[32] It is clear that the Asteraceae were around when dinosaurs walked the Earth.

Using these dates as calibration points, we can say that the Asteraceae began to diversify several million years after the origin of the family, as the climate warmed and flowering plants diversified. Together with the present distribution of the most basal Asteraceae subfamilies,

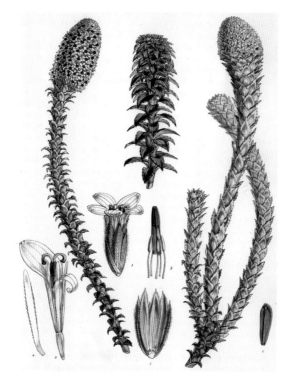

Snakeplant, a Falkland Island endemic, collected by Joseph Hooker during his exploration of the Antarctic between 1839 and 1843.

this data strongly implies that the family emerged at high latitudes in the Southern Hemisphere.

True Sunflowers and Their Relatives

The sunflower genus and its relatives are part of the largest subfamily of Asteraceae, the Asteroideae, and members of the tribe Heliantheae. This comprises approximately 1,500 species arranged in 113 genera, most of which are from the Americas.[33] Other familiar members of the tribe include the coneflowers, echinaceas, ragweeds and compass plants. The closest relative of the true sunflowers appears to be the Floridian genus *Phoebanthus*, which comprises two herbaceous species.[34]

Stereotypically, a true sunflower is a tall, annual, unbranched plant with a chrome-yellow flower head the size of a dinner plate. Fortunately, true sunflowers have much more variability than this stereotype would imply. Some are perennials with branched stems that may be as little as a few decimetres high. Flower heads vary in colour from cream through yellow and orange to red and deep burgundy, and in most species the diameter is rarely more than 15 cm (6 in.). In 1969 Charles Heiser, a North American sunflower expert, and his colleagues painted a picture of the sunflower genus as imperfectly understood, despite its familiarity, attractiveness and wide distribution.[35] Heiser had used the panoply of sophisticated techniques emerging in the 1960s to collect data, including morphological, anatomical, chemical and cytological surveys and breeding experiments. Technology presented no easy solution to the problem of delimiting and identifying sunflower species, however. Instead, the reasons why sunflower species were so difficult to tell apart were revealed: for example, ecological and developmental variability, hybridization and the peculiarities of sunflower genetics.

When efficient methods to study the structure of DNA became readily available, in the 1980s, genetic explanations were found for the problems Heiser and his colleagues had faced. Two particularly important factors in the adaptation and diversification of wild sunflowers are hybridization and chromosome rearrangement. Hybridization is a process whereby different genetic lineages are combined in single individuals, and it usually occurs when two species cross. Since the early twentieth century detailed investigations of the patterns of variation in American sunflowers have transformed our understanding of species evolution. Similarly, Soviet plant breeders released economically useful variation within the annual sunflower when they applied artificial selection in the mid-twentieth century.

Hybridization

Hybridization between plant species is thought to be common. In Britain, which has one of the best-studied floras in the world, more

Variation in the sunflower genus *Helianthus*: *H. giganteus*; *H. debilis*; *H. multiflorus*; *H. diffusus* (clockwise from top left).

than nine hundred hybrid plants have been recorded growing outside gardens and fields.[36]

Approximately 6 per cent of these hybrids are Asteraceae; many between native species or between native and introduced species. In Britain, introduction of one species has had lasting impact on the islands' Asteraceae flora: Oxford ragwort. Following the introduction of Oxford ragwort at the beginning of the eighteenth century, its range expansion, in the wake of the industrial revolution, resulted in the evolution of four new sorts of ragwort, including the endemic Welsh ragwort. Three of these speciation events involved crossing between the same pair of species – diploid Oxford ragwort and tetraploid groundsel – with the genetic outcomes being sufficiently different to be recognized as separate species. Hexaploid Welsh ragwort originated in the early twentieth century and is reproductively isolated from its parents; it remains highly localized in Wales. There was a separate evolution of Welsh ragwort in Edinburgh in the 1970s, although this lineage today appears to be extinct in the wild.[37] Much more widespread is tetraploid radiate groundsel, which was first discovered in Dublin in the mid-nineteenth century. Today it is found on wasteland in many parts of Britain. Radiate groundsel was formed when Oxford ragwort-groundsel hybrid offspring repeatedly crossed with groundsel, to produce a plant that looks similar to common groundsel with ray florets.[38] Another radiate tetraploid ragwort-groundsel hybrid, the highly localized – if not extinct – York groundsel, evolved through a slightly different genetic route.[39] York groundsel may be one of many different evolutionary experiments that happen in natural ragwort-groundsel populations; it just happened to be sufficiently distinct to attract the attention of botanists, who gave it a formal name. The fourth example is a sterile, triploid hybrid between Oxford ragwort and the introduced plant sticky groundsel. The hybrid became very common on bombsites and wasteland after the Second World War.[40]

In addition to species evolution associated with polyploidy, it is also possible for species to evolve in the absence of ploidy differences.

Much of the pioneering work on understanding so-called homoploid hybridization and speciation, where parents have the same ploidy levels, has come from research into the true sunflowers. Since the early 1980s, computer modelling, genomic mapping, experimental hybrid re-creation and investigations of evolution history have combined to reveal some of the splendid detail of evolution in the sunflower genus.[41]

In North America, three diploid hybrid sunflowers have evolved by hybridization between the common sunflower and the prairie sunflower over approximately 200,000 years. The parental species have different ecologies: the common sunflower is a plant of heavy clay soils, while the prairie sunflower occurs on dry, sandy sites. Across the mosaic of soils in the central and western United States these widespread species may come into contact with each other, producing populations of intermediate-looking plants. Each crossing event is an opportunity for a genetic experiment, and the shuffling of blocks of genes on the hybrid's chromosomes. Over tens of generations these genetic processes have stabilized to produce three species that are distinct from their parents.

The desert sunflower and dune-loving western sunflower are restricted to parts of Utah and northern Arizona, while the paradox sunflower is a salt-marsh plant of western Texas and New Mexico. Each species has many traits associated with the habitats in which it evolved. For example, the large seeds of the western sunflower prevent them from being blown away and provide a food reserve for rapid root growth; the plant's succulent leaves are thought to reduce water loss and sand abrasion. Traits associated with the paradox sunflower's saline habitat include fleshy leaves and mechanisms to reduce the uptake of toxic sodium ions.

Homoploid speciation is not restricted to the sunflowers; Oxford ragwort itself is a homoploid hybrid. Its parents are found on the slopes of Mount Etna, one species at the top of the volcano and the other at the bottom. At a few intermediate altitudes the species come into contact with each other and hybridize.[42]

Four opportunistic Asteraceae growing together next to a building site in central Oxford: groundsel; prickly sowthistle; bristly oxtongue; dandelion (clockwise from the back).

Evidence for Darwin and Wallace's great idea – evolution – has become incontestable. We can unlock the DNA code from any organism on Earth, and consequently our understanding of the tree of life has improved dramatically. We are now able to investigate the origins of species and the routes by which they have been distributed through time and space. Furthermore, we can rationally manipulate the genetics of different organisms. Intriguing questions remain about how the Asteraceae diversified and became dispersed to occupy almost every terrestrial habitat on the planet.

three
Surviving

❀

Edelweiss is not a rare plant . . . Yet if we were to set forth
in order to collect this plant, our chances of coming across
it would usually be quite small . . . Edelweiss is restricted
to the driest and barest rocks, barren of other plants; and
since such localities are relatively infrequent, the Edelweiss
is a local plant, though often exceedingly abundant where it
does occur.
Edward Arber, *Plant Life in Alpine Switzerland* (1910)[1]

Based on temperature and rainfall patterns, and soil type, there
are four broad sorts of global vegetation: tundra, forest, grassland and desert. Moving from the poles towards the equator,
just beyond the limits of the ice sheet, where temperatures are low
and seasons are short, there is tundra. As temperatures, rainfall and
season length increase, bands of coniferous and broadleaved temperate forests form, eventually giving way to subtropical and tropical
forests. Where rainfall is limited or strongly seasonal, grasslands,
savannahs or deserts form.

It is undeniable that the Asteraceae is an ecologically successful
family; there are few environments that cannot boast their share of
the family. Across every continent except Antarctica, Asteraceae occur
throughout these vegetation bands from sea level to altitudes of more
than 6,000 m (20,000 ft). Furthermore, since Asteraceae thrive in
disturbed habitats, they are ideally suited to life among humans.

Indeed, the family is likely to have been part of our lives since we started to disturb the planet with our fireplaces, fields, gardens, middens and rubbish heaps.

Many of the close relatives of true sunflowers are herbaceous, but a few, such as the genus *Scalesia*, are woody. *Scalesia* is a small genus that is endemic to the Galapagos Islands, where species have evolved in different habitats and islands across the archipelago; it is perhaps the botanical equivalent of Darwin's finches.[2] Woodiness among Asteraceae on oceanic islands abounds. She-cabbage and he-cabbage trees (which are in different genera, despite their common names) are endemic to the island of St Helena in the South Atlantic.[3] In the Pacific, the woody silverswords are endemic to Hawaii. In Macaronesia sowthistles have speciated to form at least thirty species, adapted to different islands and different habitats.[4] Darwin, in *On the Origin of Species* (1859), observed that woody plants on islands frequently belonged to otherwise herbaceous groups. In Macaronesian

Jean-François Millet, *Man with a Hoe*, 1860–62, showing a worker cultivating waste ground dominated by thistles and dandelions.

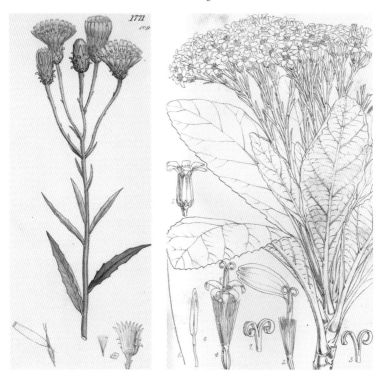

Left: Narrow-leaved hawkweed, a widespread species of north temperate regions, with complex patterns of cytological and morphological variation. *Right:* The he-cabbage tree, a woody member of the Asteraceae, endemic to the Atlantic Ocean island of St Helena.

sowthistles, woody species evolved from single colonization events by herbaceous mainland ancestors. The signature of these events is found not only in the plants' DNA, but also in their wood anatomy.[5]

The Victorian plant collector Richard Spruce was well acquainted with the broad patterns of global plant distribution that Alexander von Humboldt had identified at the start of the nineteenth century.[6] Spruce, whose eleven-year exploration of the length of the Amazon river in the mid-nineteenth century changed our understanding of northern South America and its peoples, was astonished by the way Asteraceae diversity changed with altitude:

So long as I herborised only in the plains, I could never understand how Humboldt had assigned so large a proportion of

Flower heads of the woody Canarian sowthistle, *Sonchus acaulis.*

equinoctial vegetation to Compositae, for, from the mouth of the Amazon to the cataracts of the Orinoco and the foot of the Andes . . . the species of Compositae that exist are weeds, common to many parts of tropical America . . . But in ascending the Andes, from 1200 feet [360 m] upwards, Compositae increase in number and variety at every step . . . midway of the wooded region, and especially in places where the trees form scattered groves rather than continuous woods, Compositae are more abundant than any other family . . . while on the frigid paramos no frutescent plants ascend higher . . . and as alpine herbs . . . reach the very snow-line.[7]

In the early twentieth century the North American botanist James Small went further, concluding that the Asteraceae 'seem to have been formed with the mountains by the mountains for the mountains'.[8] However, diversity among the Asteraceae is not confined to mountains. The seasonally dry *cerrado*, the world's most diverse savannah, covers the middle of South America; approximately 10 per cent of the species there are members of the Asteraceae.[9] Asteraceae is the most

The Tenerifean endemic *Argyranthemum teneriffae*, a member of the genus that has given us the garden marguerite, growing at approximately 2,300 m (7,545 ft) altitude on Teide, the peak at the centre of the island.

frequently found family across the world's deserts, making up more than 10 per cent of all desert plants; the figure doubles for Australian, South African and North American deserts.[10] In September 1811, as he explored South Africa, the naturalist and travelling artist William Burchell emphasized the point:

> The country from the Roggeveld Mountain to the northern border of the colony [Karroo Region] . . . having very few rivers, and all of these nearly dried up in the summer; quite destitute of trees and grass, but every where covered with bushes springing out of a naked red soil deprived of moisture during a great part of the year. These bushes are not more than a foot or two in height . . . and almost exclusively belong to the Natural Order of Composite flowers . . . One general cast of features, not peculiar, however, to this district, pervades all these vegetables; a minute and arid foliage.[11]

To survive such a wide range of environmental conditions, Asteraceae must protect their bud banks, or potential growing points. Buds are found all over a plant's body, especially on its stems, and may become new shoots or flowers; seeds are buds that move. In the early twentieth century the Danish ecologist Christen Raunkiær grouped plants according to the positions of their bud banks.[12] Broadly speaking, bud banks may be held high above soil level, at or near the soil surface or below its surface. Under adverse conditions, perennials therefore persist or retreat. Persisters protect their exposed buds above ground, while retreaters die back to buds held at ground level or below. In contrast, annuals invest in the next generation; their buds survive in seed banks.

If a seed finds itself in a habitat it will die, germinate or remain dormant. It is a truism that, unlike many animals, when environmental conditions became poor, plants cannot move but rather must endure. Of course, if poor conditions persist for long enough plants may adapt, but they must be capable of enduring extreme conditions.

Some of the most extreme, disturbed conditions faced by Asteraceae are associated with life at altitude, life with limited water and life with the threat of fire.

Getting Around

Independent of where plants are found, if they are to survive they must maintain or expand their populations. The simplest way for a plant to bulk up its numbers is to reproduce by bits of its body breaking off and rooting, a feature that has been exploited to great effect in the horticultural industry. Unfortunately, all such offspring will be clones, by definition genetically identical to their parents, and vulnerable to stochastic events such as disease. Genetic variation, which means that organisms are likely to have environmental resilience, is maintained by reproduction among distantly related individuals (outcrossing).

Flowers are organs to promote outcrossing; they carry reproductive structures and frequently attract pollinators by being showy and scented and offering food rewards (such as nectar or pollen). In the Asteraceae, the entire capitulum is generally the unit of attraction. However, in the case of the tiny capitula of the alpine edelweiss, pollinating flies are attracted by the foetid undertones of the otherwise honey-scented florets.[13] Furthermore, plants with bisexual florets may have elaborate ways (self-incompatibility mechanisms) to prevent individuals from mating with themselves (selfing) or with their close relatives (inbreeding).

On a summer's day in western Europe, many green lawns will become blotched with white within a few hours of dawn. The transformation is caused by the diurnal opening of the flower heads of the common daisy, whose name is derived from the Old English *daeges ēage* (day's eye). Many Asteraceae show similar behaviour: Jack-go-to-bed-at-noon is so named because the flower heads open early on summer days but are usually closed by noon. As an 'armchair exercise', Linnaeus selected Asteraceae with large, obvious heads and brightly

coloured rays and suggested that their daily opening and closing could be used to determine the time.[14] Linnaeus' list included dandelions that closed at nine o'clock, lettuce that closed an hour later, and *Crepis alpina*, which was closed by eleven o'clock. The sowthistle closed at midday, with smooth cat's ear, wall hawkweed and autumn hawkbit following at hourly intervals until three o'clock. By five o'clock, the flower heads of *Hieracium umbellata* were closed. Linnaeus never planted his novelty clock (*horologium florae*), but some botanic gardens have planted floral clocks, but as timepieces they have had limited success.[15] This is probably predictable, since periodic flower opening depends on many factors other than species, including day length and season.

The vast majority of Asteraceae are insect-pollinated, especially by butterflies, wasps and bees, flies and beetles; their reward is food.[16] However, food may not be the only reward for these invertebrates. In South African beetle daisies, sex is also on offer to male bee-flies.[17] The ray florets of beetle daisies, which vary dramatically in shape, number and colour, have black spots on them that resemble female bee-flies. Some spots fool male flies into trying to mate with them, causing the fly inadvertently to pick up pollen, which may then be carried to other flower heads.

There are also a few Asteraceae that are pollinated by vertebrates.[18] Bird pollination occurs in Hawaiian endemics such as the island-asters and the cosmos-flowered beggartick, and the Argentinian shrub *Hyaloseris rubicunda*. The tall, prickly South American shrub *Barnadesia caryophylla*, which has long, reddish, tube-shaped capitula that produce large amounts of sweet, sticky nectar, is pollinated by hummingbirds. The Venezuelan shrub *Gongylolepis jauaensis* is a rare example of a bat-pollinated Asteraceae, while all four species in the endemic southern African tree genus *Oldenburgia* are pollinated by mammals such as rodents.

Some Asteraceae release vast amounts of pollen and rely on wind to move it, including mugwort and ragweed. Wind also becomes a

Pappus of *Mutisia coccinea* fruits, a South American scrambler that produces fruiting heads up to 10 cm (3.9 in.) in diameter.

common pollination option when animal pollinators are rare. For example, Venezuelan frailejóns found more than 4,000 m (13,000 ft) above sea level are pollinated by wind; those species found at lower elevations are primarily pollinated by insects.[19] Some groups of Asteraceae, including the dandelions and hawkweeds, produce fertile seed without the need for pollination; their seed is derived entirely from female tissue through a process known as apomixis.[20]

Every successfully pollinated and fertilized floret produces a single fruit, and each capitulum may form hundreds of single-seeded fruits. Asteraceae fruits are most familiar to us as the individual structures that float away when a child blows on a dandelion 'clock' to tell the time. In Brazil, the introduced dandelion is called *amor-dos-homens* (men's love), a reference to the fruits that are blown away on a puff of wind. Since the plant spreads its fruits singly, competition among offspring, and between parents and their offspring, is minimized once sites suitable for seed germination are occupied.

Like a parachute, the pappus creates a large surface area that slows the fruit's fall, so wind can carry offspring far away from their mother. Furthermore, the fruit's structure means that it is very stable in flight. Across species there is tremendous variation in the shape, size and form of fruits. Some have little or no pappus, as in the true sunflowers. In other fruits the pappi are composed of two or more rows of hairs, or even scales or teeth. All these features, together with the height at which the fruits are released and the humidity of the air, will affect the aerodynamics of Asteraceae fruits.[21]

Walk through an area of wasteland at the height of summer and within minutes a wide diversity of Asteraceae fruits will become stuck to one's clothes by hooks, spines and barbs. Some, such as the beggar-ticks, have pappi modified into barbs, so animals are likely to be primary dispersers. In other primarily wind-dispersed species, animals play a casual role in dispersal; for example, hawkweeds have tiny teeth on their pappus hairs that may catch on passing creatures. In other cases, such as cocklebur and burdock, the unit of dispersal is not the fruit but the entire capitulum; hook- and spine-covered involucral

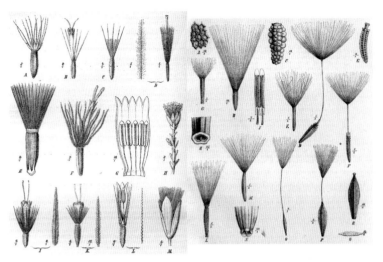

Fruit and pappus variation in Asteraceae.

bracts become caught in fur and feathers.[22] Specific adaptations to water dispersal are unusual, for example in the rare North American decurrent false aster, although wind-dispersed fruits may be accidentally carried long distances by water.[23]

Fruits that float on wind or water or hitch lifts from animals can move hundreds of kilometres across oceans to colonize islands such as Hawaii and Macaronesia. Some of the first plants to recolonize the volcanic Indonesian island of Krakatoa after it exploded in 1883 were Asteraceae.[24] However, once a plant is established on an island, there is a risk that its offspring can be moved from hospitable to hostile areas. Consequently, some species have evolved mechanisms to reduce their chances of being dispersed over long distances. Most tickseed fruits are small with claws to aid animal dispersal, but those of endemic Hawaiian tickseeds are large and lack grapples.[25] The phenomenon of island daisies being less mobile than their mainland cousins is not restricted to endemic species. Cat's ear is a widespread, northern temperate species of grasslands and waste places. Plants from cat's ear populations on western Canadian islands produce large fruits with small pappi, which reduce mobility and dispersal compared to mainland populations.[26]

Importantly, capitula need not have morphologically or physiologically uniform fruits, since diverse fruits in a capitulum may increase species' resilience to environmental change or enable them to escape unfavourable conditions. For example, the North and South American yellow-flowered wingpetal modifies its dispersal according to environmental conditions.[27] Each capitulum produces barbed and unbarbed fruits; barbs aid animal dispersal. When competition is strong or the environment becomes very dry, more barbed fruits are produced, so the next generation is more likely to escape adverse conditions. In North American camphorweed capitula, fruits have similar mass, but fruits derived from ray florets lack pappi.[28] Fruits derived from disc florets disperse further and germinate more rapidly than those from ray florets, which travel over short distances and lie dormant in the seed bank. Differences in fruit dispersal and germination from within capitula are found in other Asteraceae, including common ragwort and *Crepis sancta*.[29] The situation becomes more complex still in the Mediterranean yellow succory.[30] Two types of capitulum are produced: aerial ones and subterranean ones near the ground. The subterranean capitula produce two types of fruit, while the aerial capitula produce three, and all differ in their shape, size, mass, dispersal and germination characteristics.

Life at the top

Life at high altitude is stressful for plants, because temperatures fluctuate markedly between day and night. In the tropics, daytime temperatures may rise to more than $15°C$ ($59°F$), while night-time temperatures drop below freezing – in the words of the Swedish botanist Olov Hedberg, 'summer every day and winter every night'.[31]

Since plants are mostly water, freezing can be fatal. Imagine a plant cell as a water-filled balloon inside a cardboard box. The balloon is the cell membrane, which surrounds all the biochemical apparatus essential for life. The box is the wall, which gives the cell its rigidity. If freezing only produces ice crystals on the surface of the box there will be little effect on the balloon and its contents. However, if the water inside the balloon starts to freeze, ice crystals may puncture it. When the ice thaws, the balloon will rupture and the box will collapse, just like thawing a frozen lettuce. Consequently, plants living in environments that are prone to extreme cold have evolved mechanisms to avoid or tolerate freezing.[32]

The European edelweiss, with its distinctive clusters of tiny yellow capitula surrounded by garlands of bracts, is distributed between

The giant senecio, *Dendrosenecio johnstonii*, as depicted when the species was first described in 1887.

The frailejón, *Espeletia corymbosa*, in the Venezuelean *páramos*.

1,500 and 3,400 m (5,000–11,000 ft) above sea level, from the Pyrenees through the Alps to the mountains of the Balkan Peninsula. The entire plant has a dense covering of silvery hairs, which are adaptations to deal with three stresses commonly experienced by plants growing at high altitudes: cold, aridity and ultraviolet irradiation.[33] Asteraceae living above the treeline in the mountains of East Africa, the Himalayas and the northern Andean *páramos* reach even greater altitudes than edelweiss, but have similar ways of coping with their environments; evolution has converged on similar solutions to similar problems.

East African giant groundsels populate altitudes above 3,500 m (11,500 ft) on the arc of mountains surrounding Lake Victoria, where Kenya, Tanzania and Uganda meet. The branch tips of these stout, odd-looking trees are decorated with rosettes of large, white-haired leaves, beneath which are dense skirts of dead leaves. Giant groundsels grow slowly; trees up to 10 m (33 ft) tall may be more than 350 years old, while leaf skirts may be decades, if not centuries, old.[34] In South America, in the tundra-like *páramo* grasslands above the Andean cloud forests, an unrelated group of Asteraceae, the frailejóns, have a similar appearance to giant groundsels. The woody, palm-like frailejóns grow up to 4 m (13 ft) tall and their stems are topped by rosettes of large, thick, densely hairy leaves, below which are busby-like masses of dead, phenol-rich leaves that resist rot for decades.[35]

The central European saw-worts, *Saussurea alpina* and *Saussurea depressa*. Many members of the genus are adapted to life at high altitudes.

In such plants, buds are insulated by the layers of dead leaves and thick mats of hair. At night, as temperatures fall, outer leaves may fold over tender young leaves, forming a 'night bud'; without it, the young leaves may die. Furthermore, the sheer bulk of a rosette of leaves may act rather like a storage heater, heating up during the day and slowly releasing warmth at night. Fluids may accumulate in wells at leaf bases, covering the buds and contributing to heat storage. Mucilages in these 'rosette fluids' act as natural antifreezes. Another strategy is to delay the formation of ice crystals, allowing time for temperatures to rise and the threat from frost to disappear for another day.

In alpine Asteraceae with giant rosettes of hairy leaves, apical buds may be warmed in another way. Leaf hairs reflect heat, while the rosette shape concentrates the heat on the bud, like a radio telescope concentrating radio waves. In a silversword species that is restricted to zones above 2,000 m (6,500 ft) on two Hawaiian volcanoes, such mechanisms ensure that the buds are about 25°C (77°F) warmer than the ambient temperature.[36] Meanwhile, semi-translucent bracts surrounding the capitula of some high-elevation Himalayan saw-worts ensure that the temperature of the capitulum remains high enough for flowers and fruit to develop.[37] In another high-elevation saw-wort, the woolly surfaces of the leaves and capitula act as waterproofing or ultraviolet protection, not insulation.[38] Perhaps appropriately, the scientific name for the saw-worts, *Saussurea*, honours two men who made major contributions to our understanding of alpine environments: Horace-Bénédict and Nicolas-Théodore de Saussure.

Humans also exert major influence on Asteraceae populations over time by applying artificial selection pressures. During the twentieth century the snow lotus, a rare, high-altitude Tibetan Asteraceae, became significantly reduced in height.[39] This appears to have been a result of unconscious selection by people harvesting large specimens from wild populations for use in popular Chinese medicines. Because plants were harvested before they produced fruit, 'tall' genes were removed from the population, and 'short' genes became more prevalent in future generations. However, populations that were protected from being harvested produced taller plants than unprotected populations, probably because they retained their 'tall' genes.

Living with Water Stress

Water is fundamental to life on Earth. All plants need it to grow and reproduce. In about 1715 the Reverend Stephen Hales, a curate in Teddington (a village that is now part of Greater London), began to investigate the problem of sap movement through plants.[40] Hales was a pioneering experimentalist who had been investigating the messy business of animal blood circulation since the beginning of the century. His plant experiments were cleaner but no less enlightening than the vivisection he conducted on horses and dogs. On 3 July 1724 he began a series of experiments that would change our understanding of how plants interact with their environments.

Starting with a potted sunflower, Hales sealed the soil surface with a lead plate (which contained a tiny watering hole that could be easily corked) and sealed the rest of the pot. Comparing the amount of water added to the pot with changes in the weight of the pot and sunflower allowed him to find how much water disappeared into the atmosphere. Measuring the surface area of the plant, Hales discovered the rate of 'perspiration' (today called 'transpiration') per unit of surface area. Repeating the potted sunflower experiment at different temperatures, humidities and levels of cloud cover, Hales found that clear skies and heat increased transpiration; humidity and clouds decreased it. He went further: he showed that plants with leaves pulled up water from the soil, whereas plants whose leaves had been removed did not draw up water. He concluded that evaporation of water from the surface of leaves was sufficient to move water up the plant from the soil.

Plants must lose water if they are to move it from the soil to their leaves, through their intricate vascular system. Water is lost from leaf

overleaf: Flower head of the African xerophyte Barbary ragweed, which has thick, fleshy leaves covered in bluish wax.

Reverend Stephen Hales's sunflower experiment, which showed that water moves through a plant from the soil to the atmosphere.

The woody Macaronesian endemic Astereaceae, *verode*, in its native desert-like habitat.

surfaces through minute holes called stomata, which are surrounded by a pair of guard cells that control their opening and closing. Plants have evolved morphological and physiological strategies to cope with the dilemma of losing water in order to acquire it. These involve minimizing water loss from leaves and maximizing water uptake from the soil. Two broad strategies can be adopted. Persisters endure their conditions by having adaptations such as fleshy leaves with thick, waxy cuticles, and/or enlarged stems, such as South African kleinias and othonnas. In contrast, retreaters cope with extremes of desert life by appearing only when conditions are right; the seed bank is an ideal means of long-term survival.

Plants may face seasonal or daily (diurnal) water stress. The most obvious reason for water stress is that there is little water available, for example under desert conditions. More subtle examples of water stress are also found. Plants growing in damp soils in very windy environments are in danger of drying out since high winds increase transpiration rates.[41] Such physiological drought is also associated with cold environments, such as the *páramos*, and high transpiration during sunny periods. The stems of giant groundsels and frailejóns contain reservoirs of water so that the leaves can be supplied with water in the early morning when water in the soil may be frozen and therefore unavailable for use by the plant.[42] The spongy trunks of some Andean frailejóns capture water and release it into the soil, making significant contributions to high-altitude aquifers and lakes and eventually lowland rivers.

In Namaqualand, an arid region of Namibia and northwest South Africa about a quarter the area of the United Kingdom, the short, predictable wet season produces carpets of vividly coloured flowers, including many different sorts of Asteraceae, such as othonnas, everlastings and felicias.[43] Days after the first rains, fruits of annual Asteraceae in the soil seed bank will germinate, and within weeks they will have flowered and been pollinated to produce the next generation to replenish the seed bank. The predictability of flowering has made the blooming Namaqualand deserts a tourist attraction and, consequently, an important source of income for local people.[44]

In most plants, photosynthesis – the biochemical process by which carbon dioxide and water are converted into sugars through the action of sunlight – is mediated through the 'Jekyll and Hyde' enzyme Ribulose bisphosphate carboxylase oxygenase (RuBisCO). As Jekyll, RuBisCO adds carbon dioxide to a sugar containing five carbon atoms to produce two three-carbon molecules, which eventually produces sugars and starch. This is C_3 photosynthesis and is typical of Asteraceae in tropical or temperate areas with access to moderate amounts of water, sunlight and carbon dioxide. As temperature or water stress increases, the Hyde side of RuBisCO emerges. Instead of adding more carbon dioxide to the five-carbon sugar, oxygen is added

Flower head of the African xerophyte *Kleinia abyssinica*.

in a process called photorespiration. Photorespiration reduces the efficiency of photosynthesis.

To overcome the disadvantages of photorespiration, plants have developed different strategies to survive in hot, dry environments. Some Asteraceae have evolved a biochemical mechanism at the start of C_3 photosynthesis that keeps carbon-dioxide levels high.[45] This process is C_4 photosynthesis. At night carbon dioxide is converted to molecules containing four carbon atoms in special cells. During the day these compounds are transported into other cells, where carbon dioxide is released and C_3 photosynthesis takes place.[46]

Crassulacean acid metabolism (CAM) is another photosynthetic mechanism to cope with life in arid conditions.[47] In CAM plants, stomata remain shut during the day, which limits transpiration; they are open at night to acquire carbon dioxide. Carbon dioxide is stored as a four-carbon organic acid at night and released during the day, when it can be used in photosynthesis. Both CAM and C_4 are carbon-concentrating mechanisms, capable of making efficient use of water. They differ in that carbon dioxide is concentrated spatially in C_4 plants and temporally in CAM plants.

Playing with Fire

We learned to make and control fire some thirty to forty millennia ago, using it to harvest and cook our food, clear land, enrich soil, drive and herd game, and even as a weapon.[48] The dramatic effects of uncontrolled fires on our lives frequently make the news headlines. Plants adapted to life with fire millions of years before we even evolved, and in fact fire – a chemical chain reaction requiring fuel, oxygen and heat – is an important part of the disturbance regime of many natural habitats. During dormant periods, dry seasons and periodic droughts fuel accumulates in the form of dead leaves and stems, while lightning strikes provide the necessary spark. With a little wind, convection currents establish themselves and fire spreads across a landscape. Natural fires range from the smouldering, slow-burning

Herbarium specimens of *Helichrysum* species collected from Mount Mulanje (Malawi) in the 1980s and '90s and stored in Oxford University Herbaria; *H. nitens*; *H. whyteanum*; *H. herbaceum*; *H. buchananii* (clockwise from top left).

Lychnophora, a genus of small South American trees, frequent in the highlands of central Brazil.

types to rapidly travelling infernos with flames several metres high. The intensity of fires depends on weather conditions, topography and fuel type.[49]

Ecologically, fire is chemical grazing. Fire temperature influences seed germination, bud resprouting, soil microbes and soil nutrients. Initially, fire raises the temperature of the soil surface and removes living and dead plant material. After the fire, there will be high light levels, little competition from other plants and a nutrient-rich, warm, sterile ash in which seeds can germinate. However, some nutrients will be lost, especially nitrogen and sulphur, and wind and water erosion will increase until the surface of the soil is stabilized. Surface stabilization can start within days of a fire, as the first seeds germinate and perennials begin to resprout. For example, the Cape everlasting stands out in the fire-prone *fynbos*, a type of South African heathland, because of its pure-white capitula bracts, while chemicals in smoke or aqueous extracts of burnt wood encourage its seeds to germinate.[50]

Unlike animals, plants cannot run away from fire. Some are killed by fire and must recolonize burnt areas. However, many species in fire-prone areas are well adapted to protecting their seeds and the buds of adults from the effects of fire. In seasonal climates, fire is more likely during the dry season. Drying back during this period and resprouting with the arrival of the rains at the start of the wet season therefore reduces both water loss and fire damage. Many Asteraceae species in fire-prone lands apparently disappear during the dry season, or appear only after fire. They are well adapted to the strong seasonality of the climate and the stochasticity of fire.

The Asteraceae is one of the largest and most diverse plant families in the *cerrado* of central Brazil. Gnarled-stemmed, tree-like Asteraceae are a consequence of those buds that survive stochastic pruning by fire, while the thick, corky bark offers the buds protection.[51] The loose accumulation of dead leaves around tightly packed growing points acts as insulation and ensures that fire passes quickly over a plant. Soil is an excellent insulator, and during a fire the temperature a few centimetres below the surface will hardly rise.

Consequently, the seeds and buds of plants buried in the soil are protected from blazes. The Asteraceae of the *cerrado* show numerous underground adaptations to protect their buds.[52] In fact, in the *cerrado* a very high proportion of the living plant material is underground; in African savannahs the term 'underground forest' is sometimes used. There are numerous sorts of thickened, bud-bearing underground structures, for example xylopodia, literally 'woody feet'. Regrowth after a drought or fire requires food reserves, especially carbohydrates and nitrogen.[53] In many *cerrado* Asteraceae, the carbohydrate food reserve is inulin.

The Asteraceae's morphological, anatomical, physiological and biochemical adaptability has made it a botanical survivor. The family is not only well adapted to natural environments, but also adaptable to the environments that we have created over the last 10,000 years as agriculturalists and farmers.

four
Curing

Little by little experience, the most efficient teacher of
all things . . . degenerated into words and mere talk. For
it was more pleasant to sit in a lecture-room engaged in
listening, than to go out into the wilds and search for the
various plants at their proper season.

PLINY, *Natural History* (BOOK XXVI, II; *c.* AD 70)

Chemicals made by plants fill our lives. Some we use as food
or fuel, others we use to construct and colour our world.
Despite their capacity to feed, shelter and clothe us, it is the
power of plants to cure that captures our imagination. Yet the same
plants may also kill us. The early sixteenth-century Renaissance physician and 'father of toxicology' Paracelsus aptly summarized the
dilemma: dosage determines the outcome.

In 1960, in the Shanidar Cave in Iraqi Kurdistan, an archaeological site more than 60,000 years old, the skeleton of a middle-aged
Neanderthal male was discovered in soil that contained a high
density of pollen grains from daisy genera such as *Achillea*, *Centaurea*
and *Senecio*.[1] Given the context, archaeologists inferred that the
plants producing these grains were used in either Neanderthal burial
rituals or their medicinal practices. These conclusions, however, have
been cast into doubt by evidence showing that some Middle Eastern
rodents cache flowers; that is, they collect blossoms, probably for
food, and bury them.[2]

We may never know whether these genera were part of the Neanderthal *materia medica*, but we do know that these genera have been important in official pharmacopoeias and traditional medicines throughout Europe and the Middle East. Other familiar medicinal Asteraceae include North American echinacea and European camomile, while in recent years extracts of the Chinese annual artemisia and South American stevia have been lauded as cheap, effective antimalarials and as commercial sweeteners to alleviate global obesity respectively. Asteraceae such as ragweeds and wormwoods are less benign; both are major allergens, while ragworts are livestock killers in the temperate regions of the world.

A hint of Asteraceae chemical diversity is found in the rainbow of colours and spectrum of scents the family produces: vivid scarlet dahlias; subtle blue cornflowers; cumin-scented lavender cotton; thymol-scented artemisia; urine-scented chrome-yellow common ragwort; and spicy-scented orange marigolds.[3] This chapter introduces the chemistry of Asteraceae, how these chemicals are used by plants and how we have exploited those plants to cure, to kill and to add colour to our lives.

Plants as Medicine

Until the late nineteenth century, plants were the only major source of effective medicines. Ancient texts, including the Egyptian *Ebers Papyrus* (*c.* 1500 BC), refer to medicinal plants, while Pliny bemoaned the botanical ignorance of physicians.[4] Stories such as the Sumerian *Epic of Gilgamesh* and creation myths, including the account of the Garden of Eden in Genesis, give the impression that plants hold the keys to eternal life. There is a persistent belief, capitalized upon by conservation lobbies, that if we find the right plant-based medicines we can protect ourselves from, and cure ourselves of, disease and prolong our lives – but perhaps at the risk of overexploiting the resource.[5] The discovery that some plants do produce multibillion-dollar-earning medicines, such as vinblastine and vincristine from the rosy periwinkle and paclitaxel from Pacific yew, has tempted governments and

Floral collar from the embalming cache of Tutankhamun (c. 1336–27 BC) containing flower heads of cornflowers and *Picris*. The red linen used to make the collar was probably dyed with safflower.

industries to believe that there may be 'green gold' locked away in nature's medicine chest.[6]

We have slowly discovered the medicinal properties of plants throughout our evolution, yet the learning process has been risky. Our distant ancestors may have had help, not from their gods but from observing other animals.[7] In the early 1970s two Tanzanian chimpanzee populations were seen swallowing young leaves of *Aspilia*, a genus of yellow-flowered, tropical daisies with leaves the texture of sandpaper and covered with tiny, hooked hairs capable of scouring worms from gut walls.[8] Observations that East African bonobos and gorillas extracted and ate alkaloid-rich stem pith from the bitter-leaf shrub suggested that apes were purging themselves of internal parasites.[9]

Medicinal value has justified the scientific investigation of plants since at least the sixth century BC.[10] Most famously, the first-century AD Graeco-Roman physician Dioscorides catalogued the medicinal uses of eastern Mediterranean plants in *De Materia medica*. The earliest

known copy of this manuscript, the *Codex Vinbonensis* (AD 512), is housed in Vienna.[11] For 1,500 years the European study of plants was synonymous with the medicine and writings of the ancient duumvirate Theophrastus and Dioscorides. In the European Dark Ages the knowledge of medicinal plants declined in places of learning, although practical healing knowledge passed orally from generation to generation probably survived. As humanist ideas took hold during the early modern period, and Europe entered the Renaissance, ancient botanical knowledge, preserved in the Arab world, was once again incorporated into Western ideas.[12] Heavily illustrated printed herbals, often based on original observations from nature, allowed medicinal claims about plants to circulate among the literate.[13] Works such as Pietro Mattioli's *Commentarii* (1554) and John Gerard's *Herball* (1597) became best-sellers, apparently offering special insight into a Golden Age of medicinal botany.

For centuries, official European pharmacopoeias included members of the Asteraceae under such evocative names as *Herba cardui benedicti*, *Folia farfarae* and *Flores calendulae*. Many of these pharmacological names were incorporated into the plants' scientific names. *Herba cardui benedicti* is made from *Centaurea benedicta* (blessed or holy thistle) and was considered a panacea.[14] The polysaccharides in the leaves of *Folia farfarae*, derived from *Tussilago farfara* (coltsfoot), were used as an expectorant, while *Flores calendulae*, derived from *Calendula officinalis* (marigold), was used to induce sweating and as a stimulant.[15]

The study of plants in ancient China paralleled that in Europe, but there was no equivalent of Theophrastus. Importantly, there was no Chinese 'Dark Age', so the investigation of plants as medicines flourished uninterrupted. Consequently, thousands of plants were named, accompanied by detailed descriptions, producing a separate medical tradition to which millions in the West look today.[16]

Over the last century or more, orthodox Western medicine has moved away from its botanical roots.[17] This shift has not been

Cotton lavender, an aromatic Mediterranean shrub that is related to neither cotton nor lavender.

replicated across the globe, perhaps a consequence of poverty as much as conviction. For example, 80 per cent of people in Africa use plants directly as medicines, while in 2002 the global market for plant-based medicine was worth approximately U.S.\$60 billion.[18]

Asteraceae as Chemical Factories

The ability of Asteraceae to cure and to kill relies on the varied and complex chemicals they synthesize: so-called secondary metabolites. These chemicals, which include flavonoids, terpenoids and polyacetylenes, are concentrated in roots, bark, leaves, flowers or seeds, but they did not evolve to serve humans; we just happen to find some of them useful. In the Asteraceae, various chemical solutions evolved to cope with common biological problems, such as attracting and rewarding pollinators, suppressing the growth of competitors, deterring herbivores, and mounting a defence against fungal and microbial attack.[19]

Thousands of different flavonoids have been identified across the Asteraceae. These molecules attract pollinators, protect plants against damage from ultraviolet light and act as signalling molecules. The Asteraceae are also rich in terpenoids, a group of compounds that play essential roles in plant reproduction and defence. They are scent and flavour compounds, and contribute to the colour of flowers and fruits. A group of terpenoids called sesquiterpene lactones is particularly common in the Asteraceae. Lactucarium, the dried latex of the European bitter lettuce, has been used for centuries as a mild sedative, and is rich in sesquiterpene lactones, such as lactucin and lactucopicrin.[20] Rubber, a terpenoid polymer, is another plant defence compound. During the Second World War, when European supplies from Malaysian rubber-tree plantations dried up, rubbers from the taproots of Russian dandelions and the stems of the Mexican guayule shrub were used as substitutes.[21] Although Asteraceae rubbers were wartime stopgaps, they are today being investigated once more, this time as specialist hypoallergenic rubbers for gloves and condoms.[22]

Garden marigold, a plant widely cultivated for its ornamental, medicinal and culinary properties.

The Dalmatian chrysanthemum, with its distinctive white-and-yellow inflorescences, is native to a narrow strip of the Adriatic coast from Croatia to Albania.[23] This species is a source of the terpenoid pyrethrin, which – despite being a powerful insect neurotoxin – is perhaps the safest insecticide known, being non-toxic to mammals. Pyrethrin is concentrated in fruit walls and appears to prevent damage from insects. Other plants, such as the South African Cape marigold, contain cyanogenic glycosides, which combine sugar and cyanide molecules. When plants are damaged, enzymes are produced that break down the glycosides to release cyanide and deter grazers, such as insects and molluscs.

Polyacetylenes are another class of compound common in the Asteraceae, especially in the tribes Cardueae, Senecioneae, Astereae and Anthemideae. These are insecticidal and antimicrobial compounds; some are even thought to be produced in response to fungal attack. Polyacetylenes make the fruits of African marigolds and beggarticks black, and are responsible for the toxicity of plants that are used as fish poison such as *Ichthyothere terminalis* and *Clibadium sylvestre*.[24]

Alkaloids are complex, bitter, physiologically active nitrogen-containing compounds that are restricted to three Asteraceae tribes (Senecioneae, Eupatorieae and Cardueae). The most important of these are the pyrrolizidine alkaloids, some of which are highly toxic or carcinogenic.[25] Furthermore, pyrrolizidines have evolved many times in the Asteraceae.[26] In common ragwort, they are generally effective against grazing animals. However, at least one species – the day-flying cinnabar moth – has evolved to use the ragwort's own toxins to protect itself.[27] The orange-and-black-banded caterpillars eat ragwort leaves and accumulate high levels of bitter-tasting pyrrolizidines, which persist to adulthood. Consequently, the distinctive red-and-black adults are rarely eaten; predators learn to recognize them as toxic.

Other insects use the chemistry of Asteraceae in more subtle ways. In North America, particular male gall wasps subvert the chemistry of the compass plant and prairie dock as surrogate pheromones to locate their mates.[28] Wasp larvae feed and overwinter inside the flowering stems. The following spring, males emerge and must find a female. They do so by detecting a particular mixture of monoterpenes that the plants produce in response to infestation by female gall wasps. Furthermore, female wasps are able to modify the precise chemical mixture to make the plants more attractive to males.

Asteraceae in Medicine

Cultures across the planet have discovered the diverse acute, chronic or even mutagenic effects numerous chemicals in the Asteraceae have on the human body, for example as analgesics, cardiac depressants, respiratory stimulants or muscle relaxants.[29] However, interpreting the effects of plant medicines, especially the way in which they are reported, depends on understanding often culturally based concepts of illness.[30] Uncritical lists of the medicinal properties of plants litter the ethnobotanical literature, often with little indication

Dalmatian chrysanthemum, one of the sources of the commercially important pyrethrum.

of how plants should be prepared to elicit a particular effect. Plants appear to gain kudos as medicine from being used by cultures temporally or spatially distant from one's own. Antiquity or ethnicity may also bring unwarranted respectability to a plant's use, which, in the context of herbal medicines, can be lethal or at best breed false hope.[31]

In early modern Europe, practical knowledge of medicinal plants passed from generation to generation through written or oral traditions, and was augmented by the rediscovery of Hellenic thought and detailed observations of the (at times grisly) effects of plant extracts on the human body. Such pragmatic advances were sometimes allied with more unusual approaches to finding out about medicinal plants, at a time when mysticism and magic were taken seriously by individuals, as well as by states, churches and legal systems. Two of the most (in)famous ways to divine medicinal value were the Doctrine of Signatures and astrology.

Under the Doctrine of Signatures, a plant's form dictates the ailments it cures: 'God hath imprinted upon the Plants . . . in Hieroglyphicks, the very signature of their Vertues.'[32] In contrast, adepts of astrological botany believed that plants were influenced by the stars and the planets, and were merely pawns in a celestial game played for the benefit of humans. Advocates even claimed the gods had placed plant-based cures in regions where particular illnesses were endemic.[33]

Paracelsus was a powerful advocate of the Doctrine of Signatures, while the English herbalist John Gerard was proud of his skill in having discovered the 'properties and privie marks' of thousands of plants: a veritable botanical Champollion.[34] However, it was the sixteenth-century Italian genius Giambattista Porta, in the many editions of *Phytognomonica* (1588), who presented the Doctrine in its most expansive form; Porta had a fertile imagination when it came to divining associations between human ailments and plant forms.[35] For example, the typical daisy-like inflorescence was equated with the eyes, so daisies cured eye conditions, while the resemblance of

Yellow-flowered compass plant growing in Canada, covered in white-flowered prickly cucumber.

great leopard's bane root to the scorpion meant it must be useful against the animal's sting.

John Parkinson rejected such mysticism, only to be criticized by the colourful apothecary and astrological botanist Nicholas Culpeper: 'neither Gerrard [sic] nor Parkinson . . . ever gave one wise reason for what they wrote, and so did nothing else but train up young Novices in Physick in the School of Tradition, and teach them just as a Parrot is taught to speak.'[36] Culpeper was notorious as a thorn in the flesh of mid-seventeenth-century orthodox physicians, 'a company of proud, insulting, domineering Doctors, whose wits were born

Mugwort, a common member of the genus *Artemisia*.

above five hundred years before themselves'.[37] He considered himself to be guided by reason and to surpass all his predecessors, despite the fanciful justifications for his astrological beliefs. For example, 'Wormwood is an Herb of *Mars* . . . What delights in Martial places, is a Martial Herb; but Wormwood delights in Martial places (for about Forges and Iron Works you may gather a Cart load of it) *Ergo* it is a Martial Herb.'[38] Culpeper's work is riddled with ramblings on the virtues of wormwood, an apparent panacea relieving everything from conditions of the right eye in men and the left eye in women through freckles, sunburn and sore throats to French pox (syphilis) and even the trauma of childbirth.[39]

Culpeper's contemporaries were unconvinced. William Coles poured vitriol on him, maintaining that he 'understood not those Plants he trod upon', and dismissed the astrologers with a subtle theological argument: according to Genesis, plants were created on the third day and planets on the fourth, therefore astrological botany was ridiculous since cause cannot follow effect.[40]

Beliefs and stories about the therapeutic value of particular plants are persistent, even when objective evidence indicates that such cures are ineffective. However, quaint folklore surrounding plant use may have scientific bases. In 1971 the Chinese chemist Tu Youyou purified an extract from annual artemisia that was effective against the malaria parasite, and eventually a pure chemical, artemisinin, was isolated. Professor Tu made the necessary breakthrough in how to use annual artemisia by studying texts on ancient Chinese medicine.[41] In 2015 she was co-recipient of the Nobel Prize in Physiology or Medicine for her work on artemisinin and malaria. Generally, apparent hit-and-miss medicine of the past, based on undefined chemical mixtures from whole-plant nostrums – medicines that are generally considered to be ineffective or untested – has given way to pure compounds in orthodox Western medicine.

Chinese annual artemisia is today used as a source of antimalarials.

Few modern drugs have been derived from the Asteraceae compared with families such as the Apocynaceae (such as vinblastin), Rubiaceae (including quinine) or Solanaceae (such as atropine). Asteraceae-derived drugs, approved by the United States Federal Drugs Administration, include the sweetener stevioside, isolated from stevia; silymarin from blessed milk thistle, to protect liver cells; and the taste-inhibitor cynarin, isolated from the artichoke. Currently, the genus *Artemisia* is yielding particularly interesting medicinal compounds, especially antiparasitic chemicals derived from artemisinin, including artemether and artesunate, while tarragon produces the antiglaucoma agents latanoprost and bimatoprost.

The problem is how to separate robust scientific evidence about plant medicines from the cacophony of old wives' tales, since scientific drug testing is expensive, ethically sensitive and time-consuming. One approach is to modify the structures of compounds with known effects, producing families of closely related molecules that may vary in their efficacies: chemical modification. Another approach, the relative fashionableness of which has oscillated greatly since the mid-twentieth century, is to search for biologically active chemicals 'in nature': bioprospecting. Chemical modification has not produced the rewards that were predicted, while bioprospecting is time-consuming and fraught with its own ethical problems. Explicit analyses of evolutionary relationships among drug-producing plants, together with ethnobotanical data from different parts of the world, have shown that similar groups of plants are used to treat similar medical conditions.[42] This data implies that compounds in groups of traditional medicinal plants may be useful starting points for the process of discovering drugs.

Once basic research is complete, and a candidate compound with biological effects is discovered, detailed investigations are needed to convince sceptical regulators, doctors, insurance companies and healthcare funders that the compound is safe and effective and represents good value for money. Initial, preclinical investigations use cell cultures and laboratory animals to determine whether the compound is safe for clinical (human) trials. Once results have been independently reviewed, clinical trials may be approved; they are usually phased, starting with small groups of healthy volunteers before moving to large groups of patients. The results of these trials are then submitted to regulators for review, and, if accepted, the drug is licensed and marketed, although its use will continue to be monitored. Out of thousands of candidate compounds entering the initial stages of testing, only one will be approved.[43] The whole process may take a decade and cost billions of dollars, and so pharmaceutical companies must have strong intellectual property protection on new drugs. Without such protection, they could not afford the necessary tests to obtain formal approval. Furthermore, since companies must make money they tend to target drugs for common conditions. For drugs discovered using traditional knowledge, that may have accumulated over centuries, mechanisms must also be in place to enable the guardians of such knowledge to benefit financially.[44]

Ineffective medicines put people's lives at risk. Therefore, drug trials must be as rigorous and impartial as possible. The gold standard of such trials is the randomized controlled trial, in which participants are allocated randomly to either a treatment or a control group.[45] Members of the treatment group get the medicine and members

Opening flower head of the pale purple coneflower.

of the control group do not; otherwise, all members of the trial are treated similarly. This type of trial eliminates the placebo effect, while ensuring that neither patient nor doctor knows which group a patient is in, eliminating unconscious bias as much as possible.

Concentrations of biologically active chemicals inside individual plants may vary among species, across seasons, within populations and across plant parts. Consequently, predicting the specific biological and medicinal activities of whole-plant extracts is a lottery, leading to highly variable results even in controlled medical trials.[46] Such variability may raise doubts about the efficacy of whole-plant herbal extracts such as echinacea, and discredit the search for new medicinal compounds among traditional pharmacopoeias. Controlled, scientific evaluation of whole-plant extracts as medicines is a particular challenge for evidence-based medicine.[47]

Allergens and Killers

In the Western world approximately two people in every hundred suffer from plant-induced contact dermatitis.[48] Almost 19,000 plant species, most of them Asteraceae, cause the condition. Of particular concern are sesquiterpene lactones, which have parts of their chemical structure that can modify human skin proteins.[49] Since people constantly come into contact with Asteraceae – for example, as salad ingredients, ornamental plants or weeds – effective methods have been developed to test for contact dermatitis. One approach uses mixtures of chemically pure sesquiterpene lactones, while another uses whole-plant extracts of commonly grown Asteraceae such as arnica, German camomile, feverfew, tansy and yarrow.[50]

Hayfever is a common allergic reaction that occurs when certain people are exposed to proteins on the outside of Asteraceae pollen.[51] In sensitive people, even a few pollen grains per cubic metre of air produce severe symptoms. Fifty per cent of all hayfever cases in North

French marigold, a native of Central America that has been widely planted in Europe since the 16th century.

America are associated with pollen from one genus: *Ambrosia*, the ragweeds.[52] Ragweeds form high-density populations in disturbed areas, and flower in late summer and early autumn, loading the air with pollen. Since the 1950s North American ragweeds have spread across Europe to become a major environmental and medical concern.[53] One reason for the recent spread of ragweed is thought to have been the political, social and economic consequences of the fall of the Berlin Wall, which led to large-scale abandonment of agricultural land in former Eastern Europe in the 1990s.

Asteraceae allergies make life miserable for people, while Asteraceae that kill livestock have severe economic effects. Common ragwort, with its flat heads of yellow, daisy-like inflorescences, is native to Eurasia and a familiar sight in fields and on roadside verges. In Britain, it attracts emotional headlines as a destroyer of horses. Less parochially, but more importantly, it is responsible for the annual loss of hundreds of millions of pounds' worth of pasture productivity globally. Ragwort's infamy is a consequence of hepatotoxic pyrrolizidine alkaloids (such as senecionine).

Just after the First World War, two doctors in South Africa reported that people were dying after eating wheat flour. The doctors concluded correctly that the flour was contaminated with two endemic South African ragworts.[54] Under names such as Molteno disease (South Africa), Winton's disease (New Zealand) and Pictou disease (Canada), the symptoms of pyrrolizidine poisoning in livestock had been known since the late nineteenth century; the first case of British livestock poisoning by common ragwort was reported formally in 1917.[55] Human pyrrolizidine poisoning is not something of the distant past, though; in the early 1990s northern Iraqi Bedouins were poisoned when they accidentally ate groundsel fruit, while Asteraceae contamination poses a serious risk in some herbal remedies.[56]

Heavy infestations of ragwort reduce the productivity of pasture through competition with grasses and other herbs. Livestock generally avoid ragwort because of its bitterness, but they will eat it when it is dried in hay.[57] In early to mid-twentieth-century Europe, as horses gave way to petrol and diesel engines as the primary means of transport and rural power, ragwort infestations shifted from being an economic problem to one of animal welfare. In the British Isles, the Weeds Act (1959) and the Ragwort Control Act (2003) provide a legal framework to control the spread of ragwort. However, given the economic and emotional reactions engendered by ragwort poisoning, especially in horses, it is unsurprising that it is difficult to find objective information about animals specifically killed by ragwort.

As might be expected for such a common, reviled plant, ragwort is known by dozens of different local names.[58] One name, staggerwort, which describes a symptom of livestock suffering from ragwort poisoning (the staggers), is in fact derived from the fact that it was once used as a remedy for that very affliction.[59] Some show a more benign, aesthetic view of the plant. Its beauty was immortalized by the English poet John Clare in 'The Ragwort' (1831) and in the 1920s by Cicely Mary Barker as one of her flower fairies. Under its Manx name, *cushag*, ragwort also has the accolade of being the Isle of Man's national flower. One opportunistic British farmer even claimed that he had duped 'townies' into buying common ragwort as an ornamental plant.[60]

Colouring our Lives

Colours are important.[61] We use them to record our doings and ideas, dye our textiles, decorate our bodies, paint our world, express our emotions and generate wealth. Through their practical skill, pre-industrial dyers, the ancestors of today's applied chemists, discovered how to transform and manipulate plant chemicals into high-value, portable pigments. Scientific plant names that include words such as *tinctorum* ('of the dyers') or *tinctorius* ('use for dying') are reminders of an age of plant-based dyes.

Blue, yellow, red and black pigments extracted from woad, weld, madder and oak are widely known. Yellow, orange and red pigments extracted from Asteraceae, such as black mint, golden tickseed, safflower, saw-wort and yellow camomile, or the indigo-like dye from *anil de Pernambuco*, are less well known.[62] Until the development of twentieth-century aniline dyes, the thistle-like annual safflower was an important dye plant in Asia and North Africa. Safflower, naturally distributed from southwest to central Asia, appears to have originated in cultivation through the domestication of a wild, weedy species common throughout the region.[63]

The deep orange-red petals of the safflower contain low concentrations of pigments. Yellow safflower pigments are unique, water-soluble flavonoids; the red pigments are mainly water-insoluble carthamin.[64] As the flowers age, carthamin increases in abundance. The mature flower heads are harvested and dried, and the intricate process of extracting the pigment begins. To stain 1 kg (2 ⅕ lb) of cotton bright crimson, the flowers from 1–5 ha (2½–12⅓ acres) of safflower must be harvested.[65]

Prolonged steeping of the flowers in acidified water removes the yellow pigments, which are used to dye wool, silk and cotton. The remaining floral pulp is shaped into blocks and dried for storage or mixed with soda ash to dissolve the carthamin. Red carthamin, precipitated from this alkaline solution by the addition of vinegar or lemon juice, is used to dye fibres and is incorporated into paints and cosmetics. These processes require careful control if the best quality pigments are to be extracted. Consequently, the skill of safflower farmers and dyers is crucial for the profitable production of dye.

Safflower pigments have been used since antiquity to colour textiles, cosmetics and food.[66] Safflower dye has been identified from Mesopotamian cuneiform inscriptions and Egyptian textiles some 4,000 years old. Garlands of safflower adorn mummies from the Eighteenth Dynasty, while its fruit was found in Tutankhamun's tomb.[67] Outside Egypt, the oldest known scientifically authenticated examples of safflower dyes are on textiles from eighth-century AD Japan.[68] Japanese geishas used bright-red safflower pigment to paint their lips, while the same pigment, mixed with rice flour, was used in Japanese printing ink.[69] In Britain, safflower's red dye stained the cotton tape that was used to tie up legal briefs, giving us the phrase 'red

Bastard saffron or safflower, an ancient source of oil and pigment.

tape', while safflower's yellow dyes were substitutes for true saffron, giving the plant its other common names, bastard or dyer's saffron.[70] Yet safflower never attained the same status as weld or madder for producing yellow and red dyes respectively.

Even if plant chemicals have useful medicinal properties, vast, long-term investment is necessary to realize the economic rewards. However, 'winners' are very rare; in the Asteraceae, the current short-term moneymakers may be annual artemisia and stevia. International agreements have established that countries have sovereign rights over plants in their territories and over the traditional knowledge associated with those plants. However, unless agreements to protect those rights are enforced, suspicion will remain that bioprospecting and biopiracy are synonymous.

five
Feeding

Almost all we see, and touch, and taste, and smell, eat and drink, are clad with, and defended [by] . . . is furnished from that Great and Universal Plantation.

JOHN EVELYN, PREFACE TO *Acetaria: A Discourse of Sallets* (1699)

Until the mid-twentieth century, the most important culinary member of the sunflower family was the Eurasian lettuce, ambiguously caricatured by the American wit Ambrose Bierce as God's gastronomic reward to the good and punishment to the wicked. During the twentieth century the supremacy of lettuce among the Asteraceae was challenged by North American sunflowers, which emerged from horticulture into agriculture to become important sources of oil and protein. Eurasian endive and chicory found homes as bitter leaf vegetables and ersatz coffee respectively.

Among the more bizarre plant parts we consume are Eurasian globe artichokes and cardoons. Dahlias, usually thought of as ornamentals rather than food, have tubers that have been consumed by the inhabitants of their native Mexico. It is the tubers of their cousins, South American yacón and North American Jerusalem artichoke, that have wider culinary appeal.[1] Jerusalem artichoke lost the race for global acceptance to the potato, but it continues to produce flatulence in some, delight in others and etymological confusion in all.

Besides bitter herbs, the Asteraceae provides aromatic herbs that enliven food and drink, such as tarragon, alecost, *shungiku* and

103

Uses of Asteraceae: black sunflower fruits, hulled kernels and oil, tarragon, stevia and camomile, artichoke hearts and red, safflower-dyed tape.

camomile. Most notoriously of all, the family flavours *la fée verte*, absinthe, a drink associated with the spirit of artistic and political revolution in nineteenth-century Europe and the decadence of *fin de siècle* France.

Besides their use as food, thousands of cultivated and wild members of the family are essential homes and food for pollinating insects. They provide – if we are to use currently fashionable jargon – essential ecological services. The family also produces powerful insecticides to protect crops from pest damage, while some species even contain potent fish poisons.

Fertile Salad

On entering the Egyptian galleries of Oxford's Ashmolean Museum, one is confronted by a startling 2-m- ($6\frac{1}{2}$-ft-) tall fragment of a limestone statue. It is the Egyptian deity Min, whose left hand surrounds

Statuette of the Egyptian god Min from the Late Period to Ptolemaic Period (664–30 BC).

a hole below which hangs a large, well-filled scrotum. More than five millennia ago, at Koptos in Upper Egypt, centre of the fertility cult of Min, the statue would have been at least 4 m (13 ft) tall, sporting an enormous, erect wooden phallus. Images and sculptures of Min are often accompanied by a leafy plant, interpreted by scholars as a Romaine-like lettuce.[2] Unfortunately, other than a few fruits, no

Selection of lettuce grown in Europe at the end of the 19th century: 'Curled Californian lettuce', 'Beauregard lettuce', 'Aleppo Cos lettuce' (top row); 'black-seeded Bath Cos lettuce', 'Tom Thumb lettuce', 'white Silesian lettuce' (middle row); 'Florence Cos lettuce', 'Ice drumhead lettuce', 'red winter Cos lettuce' (bottom row).

physical remains of ancient Egyptian lettuces have been reported by archaeologists.[3] In the absence of physical evidence, and with botanically poor depictions of the plant, the identification of this plant as lettuce must remain conjecture.

It is tempting to speculate that the association between lettuce and male sexual potency emerged from the observation that when lettuces are damaged they bleed white, semen-like milk. Lettuce milk is the derivation of its scientific name, *Lactuca* ('milky plant'). Many other Egyptian plants ooze white sap when cut, but apparently did not elicit the same veneration.

Ancient Greek and Roman literature is replete with references to the diversity of lettuces, their culinary uses and their laxative and soporific properties.[4] In first-century AD Rome, Caesar Augustus erected an altar to lettuce after attributing his recovery from a serious illness to the plant: 'Some think your commendation you deserve,/

'Cause you of old *Augustus* did preserve./ Why did you still prolong that fatal breath,/ That banish'd *Ovid*, and was *Tully*'s death?'[5] In the third century the usually frugal emperor Tacitus refused to give up the luxury of lettuce.[6] With characteristic venom, the Roman poet and epigraphist Martial recommended the plant as a laxative and beauty treatment: 'use lettuces . . . for you have a face like one suffering from constipation.'[7] He also complained about changes in Roman habits of eating lettuce: 'Tell me why lettuce, which used to close the repasts of our forefathers, now commences our feasts?'[8] Was this perhaps so that guests could clear their bowels before the meal, or did sleepy guests consume less food, making feasts cheaper for parsimonious hosts? Most enigmatically of all, the first-century Greek historian Plutarch asked 'why women do not eat the middle part of lettuce'; unfortunately the answer has been lost.[9]

In seventeenth-century Europe, lettuce was no longer an aphrodisiac; quite the opposite. John Parkinson held that lettuce 'bound . . . to the cods [testicles] . . . helpeth those that are troubled with the Colts evill [genital inflammation]. If a little camphire be added, it restraineth immoderate lust.'[10] John Gerard stated that the 'juice of [garden] Lettuce cooleth and quencheth the naturall seed if it be too much used', while wild lettuce 'seed taken in drinke . . . hindreth generation of seed and venereous imaginations'.[11]

By the end of the century John Evelyn was planning a grand compendium of horticultural lore and practice, the *Elysium Britannicum*.[12] The manuscript was never completed, although he published one of the chapters as a paean to salads, *Acetaria: A Discourse of Sallets* (1699). Evelyn praised lettuce as a panacea 'so harmless that it may safely be eaten raw in Fevers; for it allays Heat, bridles Choler, extinguishes Thirst, excites Appetite, kindly Nourishes, and above all, represses Vapours, conciliates Sleep, mitigates Pain; besides the effect it has upon the Morals, *Temperance* and *Chastity*.'[13]

In Stuart England, gardeners apparently had a limited appreciation of the diversity of lettuce. Parkinson emphasized that there are so many sorts, and so great diversitie of Lettice, that I doubt I shall scarce be beleeved of a great many . . . some [are] of little use, others of more, being more common and vulgar; and some that are of excellent use and service, which are more rare, and require more knowledge and care for the ordering of them.[14]

He goes on to mention lettuce varieties such as red and white Romaine, Virginia, common Lumbard, Venice, Cabbage, Curled, Flanders Cropers and winter lettuce. Evelyn adds varieties such as Alphange of Montpelier, Arabic, Ambervelleres, Belgrade, Capuchin, cross-lettuce, Genoa, Imperial, Lop, French Minion, Oak-leaf, Passion, Roman, Shell and Silesian.[15] Gerard at least recognized that some of these differences were caused by the conditions under which lettuces were grown: 'by manuring, transplanting . . . the leaves of the artificiall Lettuce are oftentimes transformed into another shape.'[16] Such horticultural manipulations are likely to have been more successful at changing the appearance and taste of lettuce than watering with honey and wine, as was recommended by the fourth-century BC Greek philosopher Aristoxenus.[17] By the end of the nineteenth century French seed merchants were offering more than a hundred different types of lettuce for sale, and lettuces were available throughout the year as different cultivars came into season during the winter, spring and summer months.

Garden lettuce evolved from a group of very closely related, bitter wild lettuce species distributed around the Mediterranean Basin and southwest Asia.[18] Early farmers concentrated on selecting lettuces with low bitterness, although there is evidence that lettuce may also have been selected as an oilseed.[19] As we selected different forms, our relationship with lettuce evolved.

Venerated as priapism-promoting vegetables by the cult of Min, the plant's supposed soporific properties became a plot device in Beatrix Potter's *The Tale of the Flopsy Bunnies* (1909). In Potter's tale, some sleeping young rabbits are captured by the gardener Mr McGregor

'Lactuca sylvestris',
wild lettuce, as depicted
by Leonard Fuchs in
his herbal of 1542.

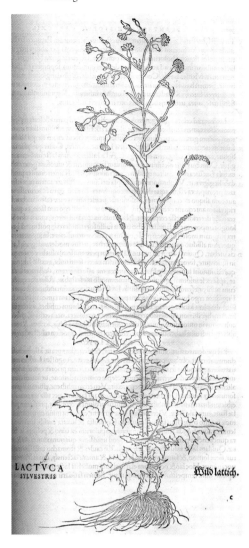

after they have been eating lettuce. He intends them for the pot, but they are saved by Benjamin and Flopsy Bunny and Thomasina Tittlemouse. Lettuces fill supermarket vegetable aisles, bulk out salads and are marketed as health foods. They are caricatured as boring, a garnish for more interesting fare, or relegated to stereotypical 'rabbit food'. However, lettuce is the most widely consumed salad leaf on the planet, despite having little nutritional value.[20] In 2013 nearly 25 million tonnes of lettuce were produced globally, most within a limited range of commercial varieties, such as 'Cos' and 'Iceberg'.[21]

Swine Food

A weedy, daisy-like plant used as a leaf vegetable in parts of South America briefly became known as Kew weed when it spread from the Royal Botanic Garden in the late nineteenth century.[22] Today this plant is called gallant soldier, a mishearing of the plant's scientific name, *Galinsoga*. A similar linguistic quirk operates with the Jerusalem artichoke, a relative of the sunflower.

The name Jerusalem artichoke was reported in seventeenth-century England, barely three years after the vegetable's European debut, and fewer than twenty years after it was first seen by Europeans in North America.[23] The apothecaries John Parkinson and Thomas Johnson were exasperated: 'We in England, from some ignorant and idle head, have called them Artichokes of Jerusalem, only because the roote . . . taste[s] like the bottome of an Artichoke head.'[24] Furthermore,

> one may wel . . . perceive, that those that vulgarly give names to plants, have little either judgement or knowledge of them: for this plant hath no similitude in leafe, stalke, root, or manner of growing, with an Artichoke, but only a little likenesse of taste in the dressed root; neither came it from Jerusalem, or out of Asia, but out of America.[25]

'Jerusalem' is apparently a corruption of the Italian *girasol* (sunflower). The law of Hobson-Jobson has taken over; no amount of explanation will change popular opinion once usage has been established.

Jerusalem artichokes are rather knobbly, potato-like tubers with thin, pale skins varying in colour from white to yellow, often becoming reddish or bluish with age; they are 'bunched or bumped out many waies, sometimes as big as a mans fist, or not so big, with white noses

German porcelain perfume burner in the form of a globe artichoke, c. 1766.

or peakes where they wil sprout or grow the next yeare'.[26] Jerusalem
artichokes have a reputation for being highly productive, even in poor
soils, but a tendency to become weedy if not carefully managed. In
1617 the English botanist John Goodyer received two artichoke tubers
from a Frenchman living in London, Jean de Franqueuill. He planted

Jerusalem artichoke, a familiar 18th-century food plant.

one of the tubers in a Hampshire garden and was rewarded with a peck (9 litres/2 gallons) of crop, which he apparently used to stock the rest of the county.[27]

Jerusalem artichokes, like their edible relatives the dahlias, are rich in inulin, a fructose polymer that belongs to a class of dietary fibres called fructans. However, inulin cannot be broken down by enzymes in the human gut. Consequently, inulins have become important in low-calorie foods, as sources of dietary fibre, for managing blood-sugar levels in diabetics and for enhancing gut flora. Unfortunately, a proportion of the population suffers from side effects associated with inulin consumption: excessive growth of methanogenic bacteria in the gut, leading to flatulence. Goodyer was evidently inulin sensitive; he said that 'which way soever they [Jerusalem artichokes] be drest and eaten, they stirre and cause a filthy loathsom stinking winde within the body, thereby causing the belly to be pained and tormented; and are a meat more fit for swine, than men.'[28]

Native Americans used the tubers, throughout the species' native range, especially as a famine food, and were cultivating them before the French explorer Samuel de Champlain visited the region around Cape Cod, Massachusetts, in 1605.[29] However, some seventeenth-century botanical cataloguers, and later Carolus Linnaeus, were confused about the geographic origin of the plant, sometimes placing it as far south as Peru or Brazil.[30] Despite assertions by the nineteenth-century American botanist Asa Gray that the evolutionary origin of the Jerusalem artichoke was 'well nigh settled', arguments continued throughout the twentieth century.[31] In 2014, using a sophisticated approach to search the species' entire genetic material, together with an intimate knowledge of sunflower biology, a team of North American researchers reported that the Jerusalem artichoke apparently evolved on multiple occasions through complex hybridizations between two other sunflower species; it was one of very few crop plants to have originated in North America.[32]

Independent of Goodyer's view, Jerusalem artichokes, or Canadian potatoes, became a popular food in the seventeenth century, at least among the wealthy: 'Some boile them in water, and after stew them with sacke [fortified wine] and butter, adding a little ginger. Others bake them in pies, putting Marrow, Dates, Ginger, Raisons of the sun, Sacke, &c.'[33] However, Parkinson was concerned that they were losing their exclusivity: 'Whereas when they were first received among us, they were dainties for a Queene . . . the too frequent use, especially being so plentifull and cheape, hath rather bred a loathing then a liking of them.'[34]

The loathing evidently triumphed as other, more palatable foods, such as potatoes, became available. The consumption of Jerusalem artichokes declined, but did not cease. The nineteenth-century Palestine soup, based on Jerusalem artichokes, perpetuated old misconceptions, while names such as sunroot and sunchoke are twentieth-century marketing devices. Jerusalem artichoke transformed into liquors such as topinambur – its name itself a misattribution of a Brazilian Amerindian name adopted in parts of seventeenth-century Europe – is an exclusive luxury.

Recently, as the realization grows that current global food supplies may not keep up with population increase in the teeth of climate change, limited political and economic will has emerged to (re-) discover new food sources, such as the Jerusalem artichoke.[35] Similar drivers have led to dreams that inulin could be converted directly into ethanol, and therefore fuel.[36]

Eating Thistles

Donkeys have famously robust constitutions; Eeyore, the depressive donkey in A. A. Milne's *Winnie the Pooh* (1926), was particularly fond of thistles. Such fondness is immortalized in the scientific name for cotton thistles, *Onopordum* ('donkey fart'), which refers to the belief that excessive consumption of these thistles causes flatulence. Popularly, the Old English word 'thistle' refers to spiny, herbaceous members of the sunflower family, especially the subfamily Carduoideae.

Despite their armature, for thousands of years we have chosen to eat the stems, flower heads and underground parts of 'thistles' such as purple milk thistle, blessed milk thistle, woolly thistle, carline thistle and burdock.[37] The eighteenth-century chronicler of the Scottish flora, John Lightfoot, reported that the Scotch thistle 'may be eaten in the same manner as [globe] artichokes and cardoons'.[38] In Britain, a once-popular soft drink, dandelion and burdock, was made by combining extracts from these eponymous Asteraceae.

People may have been forced to eat wild thistles when food was scarce or no better fare was available. However, the immature flowering heads and leaf stalks of the globe artichoke and cardoon thistles have been actively cultivated, domesticated, bred and consumed for centuries.[39] Globe artichokes are familiar in greengrocers as large, scaly, green-purple heads. Two parts of these inflorescences are usually eaten freshly cooked or preserved in oil: the fleshy bases of the involucral bracts and the fleshy receptacle upon which the florets sit. In the case of cardoons, young leaf stalks are usually blanched like celery and eaten raw or cooked.

Whether wild cardoons, cultivated cardoons and globe artichokes are three species or variants of a single species has been the subject

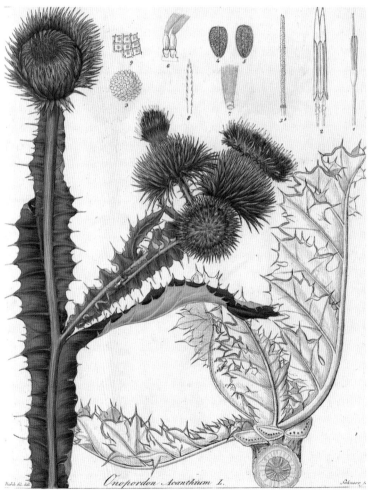

Onopordon Acanthium L.

Cotton thistle, a former food plant and currently popular garden plant.

Globe artichoke in flower. The bracts and base of the immature flower head are eaten.

of decades of discussion. The current view is that they are one species made up of three variants.

Wild cardoon, the ancestor of both globe artichokes and cardoons, is a very spiny thistle-like plant distributed through open habitats from Macaronesia in the west, along the north and south coasts of the Mediterranean to the Black Sea in the east.[40] Cardoons and globe artichokes are domesticated wild cardoons.

Compared to wild cardoons, domesticates have few spines, and have been subject to different selection pressures. Globe artichokes have been selected for large flower heads; cardoons have been selected for huge leaves.[41] Furthermore, globe artichokes are vegetatively propagated – they must be grown from offsets – while cardoons are propagated by seed. One consequence of these reproductive differences is that there is high diversity among varieties in globe artichokes but virtually none in cardoons.

Artichokes' and cardoons' resemblance to thistles, and the confusion over the way ancient Greeks and Romans applied common names for thistle-like plants, makes unpicking references to thistles, globe artichokes and cardoons in classical literature controversial. For most of the twentieth century, the view was that cardoons were known to classical writers, while artichokes became well known only from the sixteenth century.[42] More recently, reinterpretation of the historical evidence has swung the argument in the opposite direction: artichokes were probably selected from wild cardoons in Sicily towards the start of the first millennium AD and moved through the Mediterranean region by way of trade, while cardoons were domesticated in the first half of the second millennium AD in the western part of the wild species' range.[43]

Cardoon, a relative of the globe artichoke selected for its edible leaf stalks.

Globe artichokes and cardoons have followed Europeans around the globe, and in some parts of the world they have become weeds. As Charles Darwin explored the Banda Oriental (modern Uruguay) in November 1833, he reported 'immense beds of thistle, as well as of the cardoon: the whole country, indeed, may be called one great bed of these plants . . . The cardoon is as high as a horse's back.'[44]

Bitter-sweet Herbs

Generations of plant breeders may have deprived 'rabbit food' of its bite, but bitterness is a trait that is valued in some Asteraceae. Today we hardly consume the bitter herb tansy, but that was not always the case. Before the nineteenth century tansy was a favourite seasonal flavouring, believed to be good for kidney disorders, fertility in women and the prevention of gout.[45] However, it was around Easter that it was most popular. Lenten associations apparently come from the bitter herbs of the Passover. However, religious observances during Lent had more worldly consequences, wind and worms, both of which tansy was believed to alleviate.

On 20 April 1666 Samuel Pepys met one of his numerous mistresses and, 'after a walke in the fields to the King's Head, and there spent an houre or two with pleasure', they ate a tansy.[46] In Restoration England tansy juice was popular as a flavouring for egg-rich puddings. However, by the mid-eighteenth century tansy recipes show that it was more important that the puddings were green than bitter.[47]

Chicory and endive, native European plants domesticated for their leaves and roots, are popular ingredients in the cooking of the region. Chicory root has another use: as a coffee substitute, together with the root of the dandelion. When chicory root is cut into pieces, kiln-dried and pulverized, inulins are partially broken down and caramelized, while some bitter sesquiterpene lactones are degraded. The resulting product resembles faintly liquorice-scented ground coffee.[48]

In 1850 about 5.5 million tonnes of roasted chicory were sold in Britain under names such as Mocha powder, ladies' coffee, pectoral

Flower head of chicory, whose root and young leaves are eaten.

coffee, Chinese coffee, Tom Thumb coffee, Polka coffee and colonial coffee.[49] However, Queen Victoria's coffee merchant in Edinburgh, William Law, dismissed the threat that roasted chicory posed to the coffee trade: 'It has little in common with [coffee] except its colour, and has nothing to recommend it except its cheapness.'[50]

Using chicory as ersatz coffee was a consequence of Napoleon's policy of substituting home-grown for colonial produce, while mixing chicory with coffee was a Dutch 'innovation' at the beginning of the nineteenth century. The practice was soon taken up by the French, but it was only in the early 1830s that it became fashionable in Britain.[51]

In 1820 the chemist Friedrich Accum published a book highlighting the 'fraudulent sophistications' associated with British adulteration of food.[52] One witty contemporary reviewer thanked the author 'for the great service he has done the community, by opening our eyes, at the risk of shutting our mouths for ever'.[53] However, chicory was notable by its absence from Accum's catalogue and his list of coffee adulterants.

The adulteration of coffee with chicory was effectively legalized by the British Treasury in 1840, leading to a thirteen-year Parliamentary argument among chicory and coffee producers over the rights and wrongs of protectionist versus free-trade economics, home versus foreign trade and the effect of taxation on free enterprise.[54] The coffee producers' Parliamentary champion was Thomas Anstey, Undersecretary for the Colonies. Naively, coffee producers argued that for every pound of chicory purchased they missed out on selling one pound of coffee.

The founder and editor of *Simmonds' Colonial Magazine and Foreign Miscellany*, the Jamaican coffee planter Peter Simmonds, regaled his readers with reports that the returns from the chicory were so great that chicory itself was being adulterated, before it was used to adulterate coffee. He went on to emphasize the health risks of chicory contaminants as diverse as ground parsnip, white carrot, radish, peas and beans, brick dust, earth and roasted bread and acorns.[55]

William Law was philosophical, rejecting the colonial coffee producers' arguments since coffee drinkers preferred chicory-coffee mixtures to pure coffee anyway. Ultimately, he argued, the market would decide: 'Competition amongst the [coffee dealers], and an improving taste amongst the [coffee drinkers], are the only permanent securities against the success of ultimate wrong.'[56] A compromise was eventually reached that forced coffee sellers to state whether their products contained chicory, leading to the basis of British food adulteration and trading-standards legislation.

In 1876, under the new laws, a liquid mixture of sugar, coffee and chicory was manufactured in Glasgow. 'Camp Coffee', with its distinctive label informed by the romanticism of Empire, is still marketed. The original label, with its image of an Indian servant serving coffee to a Gordon Highlander, has gradually morphed as the politics of Britain's imperial legacy have become more ambiguous. In today's label, the Indian man is seated, sharing a cup of coffee with the soldier. Suitably labelled coffee substitutes, often pure roasted chicory, are also sold under the guise of health products.

As the potato famine (1845–52) was having its destructive effect on the lives of hundreds of thousands of people in Ireland, the enthusiasm for chicory cultivation was reaching its peak. The Irish circuit judge William Seymour argued that chicory would 'prove of more substantial advantage to the labouring classes in the Emerald Isle, than many of the political "panaceas" of the day!'[57] The cultivation of chicory was never established in Ireland, however, and even the extensive chicory fields around mid-nineteenth-century York were ploughed up as advantageous tax regimes applied to home-grown chicory disappeared.

Aromatic Herbs

Aromatic plants used for flavouring have no calorific value but make food and drink more interesting. Flavourings that can be obtained from the Asteraceae include alecost (or costmary), formerly added to beer as a substitute for hops, and black mint, used in some Andean cooking. However, the most widely used culinary aromatics are the wormwoods, species of the genus *Artemisia*.

The name of *Artemisia*, a Northern Hemisphere genus of some four hundred species, commemorates the goddess Artemis. The English 'wormwood' is derived from the Old English *wermod* through centuries of linguistic evolution, as Britons came into contact with other European languages and cultures. In Germany, a similar route gave rise to *wermut*, which when taken into French evolved into vermouth, a drink originally flavoured with wormwood.

Wormwoods are fabled for their bitterness, hence the expression 'bitter as wormwood'.[58] Yet there are exceptions. French tarragon, whose elongated, delicately aniseed-scented leaves are essential in the *fines herbes* of French cuisine, is a sterile, cultivated form of widely distributed Eurasian wormwood. Being sterile, it must be propagated vegetatively. In contrast, Russian tarragon is a robust, seed-setting species that is sometimes substituted for French tarragon. However, its flavour lacks the subtlety of its French cousin.

Common wormwood, with its silvery green, heavily divided leaves and tiny clusters of yellow flowers, is one of the bitterest plants known: we would still be able to detect its bitterness if a handful of dried leaves were mashed up in an Olympic-sized swimming pool full of water.[59] The bitterness comes from a cocktail of sesquiterpene lactones that includes absinthin, anabsinthin, artabsin and matricin.

Common wormwood has been used to flavour alcoholic drinks at least since the time of the ancient Greeks and Romans.[60] European wormwood-containing spirits include Slavic *pelinkovac*, Polish *piołunówka* and Swedish *malört*, or steeped in beer and wine to produce English purl and Romanian *vin pelin*, respectively. However, it is absinthe that is the best-known and most controversial wormwood spirit.

Absinthe originated in Switzerland in the eighteenth century, but more than a century later it became strongly associated with French intellectual and bohemian life; it has been calculated that in 1910 the French drank 36 million litres (63 million pints) of it.[61] Elaborate

Vincent van Gogh, *Sunflowers* (repetition of the fourth version), 1889.

rituals, and intricate paraphernalia, were created to add sugar and water to absinthe, including special glasses and slotted spoons. The result was a milky, opalescent, pale-green *louche*.

When Vincent van Gogh killed himself, in 1890, his death became linked in people's imaginations with his predilection for the green spirit.[62] Absinthe was becoming associated with addiction and hallucinogens; the toxin was identified as thujone. By the outbreak of the First World War absinthe had been banned in the United States of America and in much of Europe.[63] At the end of the century the bans were revoked as the evidence for absinthe's psychoactive properties was re-evaluated. Today it has once again become a niche drink associated with more risqué elements of society.

six

Profiting

❀

He has been eight years upon a project for extracting sunbeams out of cucumbers . . . he should be able to supply the governor's gardens with sunshine, at a reasonable rate.

JONATHAN SWIFT, *Gulliver's Travels* (1727)

M aking money from plants means modifying – often radically – our landscape so that we can accommodate their needs. Our relationships with plants constantly change; we mould them, they mould us. The planet has been transformed as we have customized landscapes to accommodate agriculture, a crucial innovation in the evolution of many human societies.[1] Forests were razed to the ground, marshes and fenland drained, and savannahs and prairies ploughed to plant the crops and raise the livestock that we have domesticated over the last ten millennia. Currently, about one-third of the planet's land area is farmed. Demand for agricultural land and agricultural products will continue to multiply as the world's population increases to over 9 billion by 2050.[2]

Carbohydrates from grasses, cassava and potatoes, together with proteins from legumes, were the earliest foods grown by man on an industrial scale. Over the last sixty years, as sugars, fats and animal proteins have become readily and cheaply available, our diets have changed. Furthermore, the type of industrial raw material that we need has also changed. During this period, one previously under-exploited

125

group of crops has expanded its share of agricultural land: oilseed crops. Since 1961 an area of land about twice that of Yorkshire, England's largest county, has been added annually to the area of global oil crop production, more than doubling the area from approximately 114 to 290 million sq. km (44 to 112 million sq. miles).[3]

Four oil crops (in descending order of area harvested) consume the vast majority of this land: oil palm, soya, rape and sunflower. There is no evidence of long-term decline in our desire for plant oils, especially since people are now investigating whether extant plants are capable of providing viable alternative fuels for economies addicted to fossil plants and their derivatives. With a finite amount of land, the area needed for feeding us and growing our fuel will compete with places for us to live. On whatever land remains from this equation we will probably tolerate the planet's other species – until more profitable uses for the land are discovered.

Changing Needs

Current evidence shows that sunflowers were domesticated once, about five millennia ago, by people in eastern North America who preferred plants with large seeds.[4] The sunflower is one of the few major crops to have been domesticated in North America. However, active discussion surrounds the interpretation of archaeological, linguistic and literary evidence over the extent to which the sunflower was part of the daily and religious lives of cultures in pre-Columbian Mexico.[5] Another Asteraceae domesticated in North America is the herbaceous annual marsh elder, also a member of the sunflower tribe. About 4,000 years ago indigenous peoples in the central and southern United States cultivated it for its protein and oil-rich seed, but it appears to have been abandoned as a food source before the arrival of Europeans, when more palatable foods became available.[6]

In its native North American range, before the arrival of Europeans, sunflower varied in its use from being a source of food, medicine, fibre and dye to one of musical instruments and bird snares.[7] When sunflowers were introduced to Europe they were little more than garden novelties. In the early seventeenth century John Parkinson asserted that 'there is no use . . . in Physicke with us, but that sometimes the heads of the Sunne Flower are dressed, and eaten as Hartichokes [globe artichokes] are, and are accounted of some to be good meate, but they are too strong for my taste.'[8]

Over the past century the horticultural attractiveness of sunflowers has been augmented by the commercial attractiveness of their seeds as sources of oil, protein and vitamin E. Sunflower fruits, which lack dispersal structures such as the pappus, have a dry fruit wall (hull) surrounding an oily seed (kernel), covered in a thin, membranous seed coat. Popularly, but confusingly, the whole fruit (hull and kernel) is called a 'seed'; this convention is used here. In the twenty-first century the global wholesale price of sunflower seeds has been volatile. In February 2001 one tonne of sunflower seeds sold for about U.S.$600, peaking in 2007 at more than $1,600 before falling back to about $900 in October 2014.[9] Moreover, between 2001 and 2003 the gross value of global sunflower-seed production leapt from about U.S.$10 billion to more than $25 billion.[10] However, global trade in sunflower

Sunflowers ('Chrysanthemum Peruvianum maius' and 'Chrysanthemum Peruvianum minor') as a 17th-century garden plant.

seed is limited; most seed is consumed in the countries where it is produced.

Sunflower oil, which accounts for the vast majority of the sunflower's commercial worth, is very adaptable. It is an edible, almost tasteless, pale oil, with high levels of unsaturated fatty acids (especially oleic acid and linoleic acid), which are perceived as healthy alternatives to saturated animal fats. Sunflower oil is particularly popular in Europe and Russia, where it is a cheap substitute for olive oil, and is used for cooking, the manufacture of margarine and even the production of biodiesel.[11] Additional income is made by feeding the residue (cake) that remains after the oil is extracted to animals as a high-protein feed.

There are two groups of commercial oilseed sunflowers: those for oil extraction and those for direct consumption by us or our pets.[12] Oilseed types, which are by far the most important, fall into three broad subgroups: high linoleic (45–75 per cent linoleic acid), mid-oleic (55–75 per cent oleic acid) and high oleic (85–90 per cent oleic acid). Types containing medium to high levels of oleic acid produce high-quality cooking oil and are the most frequently planted. Oilseed types usually have small, black, oil-rich seeds with thin hulls, while confectionery types have large, grey-and-white-striped seeds containing little oil and with thick hulls. For confectionery types, size determines use: large seeds go to the 'in-shell' snack market; medium seeds to the kernel market; and small seeds to the pet trade.

In 2013 more than 44 million tonnes of sunflower seeds were produced, of which more than 40 per cent were grown in Ukraine and the Russian Federation.[13] Until the mid-1990s the production of sunflower seeds in the former Soviet Union was more or less steady, as was the area covered by sunflower farms; since the late 1990s there has been a rapid increase in production. In contrast, in its home continent, the American sunflower harvest contributes little to global production. Until the mid-1970s less than half a million tonnes of sunflower seeds were harvested annually in the United States. Production peaked in the late 1970s (at more than 3 million tonnes) but fell dramatically during the 1980s; there has since been some recovery. Curiously, the yield appears to be associated with geopolitics. Yield in the United States has increased steadily since 1961, but in the former Soviet Union it fell dramatically in the early 1990s (1.7 tonnes per hectare in 1989 to 0.97 tonnes per hectare in 1994). The drop in yield coincides with the break-up of the Soviet Union and the political instability it created. Before these events, Soviet farmers produced higher yields than their American counterparts. Since the mid-1990s the yield in the former Soviet Union has gradually increased once more, but it was only in 2013 that it overtook that of the United States.

Two other Asteraceae oilseeds, safflower and niger, have been at least partially domesticated.[14] These oils, although they have only a fraction of sunflower's global production, are important to the economies of Kazakhstan, India and Ethiopia. There is evidence that safflower was grown for oil at least 7,000 years ago in Syria and that niger was grown at least 3,000 years ago in Ethiopia; both oils were probably originally used for cooking and lighting.[15] Both species, like sunflower, yield unsaturated oils, which are rich in linoleic and oleic acids. There are two types of safflower, one rich in oleic acid and the other in linoleic acid; the former is used for human food, the latter for industrial purposes, such as the production of paint and biodiesel.[16] More recently, niger seed has become an important part of the seed mixes for wild and caged birds, and that has contributed to its increased cultivation outside Ethiopia and southern India.

Making Sunlight Liquid

The selection of desirable genes or the elimination of deleterious ones is essential for improving crop plants. Traditional approaches to breeding involve the manipulation of the frequencies of particular genes for useful crop traits through hybridization, and unconscious and conscious selection. Sunflower growers are proud of the dramatic changes they have achieved over the past century in both the yield and the quality of oil, entirely through traditional approaches to plant

breeding. However, the challenges posed by climate change, increasing human population and the loss of habitat have led breeders to consider complementing traditional approaches with advanced genetic technology that involves moving specific genes into crops, sometimes from very different organisms.

Interest in sunflowers as an oil crop developed slowly in most of Europe and the United States. In contrast, by 1779 the Russians were using sunflowers as an oil crop, perhaps because of edicts by the Russian Orthodox Church that the oil was not prohibited during Lent.[17] By the end of the nineteenth century oilseed and confectionery varieties had been developed in Russia.[18] At a similar time sunflower seeds were being returned to North America, probably in the baggage of Russian immigrants, not as low-yielding botanical novelties but as highly productive sunflower cultivars, such as 'Mammoth Russian'.

In the early twentieth century, the Soviet plant breeder Vasilii Stepanovich Pustovoit began raising the levels of oil in sunflower seeds without reducing yield; in 1913 seeds were approximately 30 per cent oil, but by the late 1950s that had risen to about 50 per cent.[19] Much of the change was achieved by reducing the amount of hull surrounding the kernel.[20] In the 1960s the Soviet cultivar 'Peredovik' became the basis of commercial sunflower oil production in the West. Furthermore, Soviet sunflower seeds even became part of Cold War industrial espionage as seeds were surreptitiously moved among Soviet and American plant breeders.[21]

Soviet sunflower breeders had used naturally occurring variation in the annual sunflower to make commercial progress. In the 1950s North American breeders started to cross sunflower species to exploit the yield advantages of hybrid vigour, the observation that plants derived from crossing between different generic types are more productive than their parents. However, the commercial production of hybrids requires female plants, so that all the seeds

Sunflower head.

produced by a mother plant are hybrid. Without female plants, the need to separate hybrid and non-hybrid seed would make the whole process uneconomical.

Individual plants can be slowly, meticulously and expensively emasculated; more effective is to identify genetically male sterile plants that are incapable of producing fertile pollen. In the late 1960s cytoplasmic male sterility (CMS) was discovered and the sunflower breeders' wish was granted. CMS is a consequence of interaction between genes in the nuclear and mitochondrial DNA, which means that plants cannot produce functional anthers or pollen. In the West, the development of the first CMS sunflower hybrids in the early 1970s caught the imagination of seed companies, leading farmers to plant more sunflowers.

Sunflower breeding continues in earnest today, especially as new demands are placed on farmers by the environments in which they want to grow sunflowers and by consumers who use the harvest. The advent of advanced breeding material during the last few decades has meant not only that sunflower oil yields have been enhanced, but also that oil composition has been successfully manipulated, offering the possibility of growing bespoke oils for niche markets. As with all crops, sunflowers are threatened by a gamut of pests and diseases, but insect pests are a serious threat to sunflower production only in North America, where the pests co-evolved with their native hosts. Birds are serious predators of developing seeds, but breeding to change the angle of the head can make sunflowers unattractive to them.[22]

Hybrid vigour increases seed yield dramatically, but yield may also be improved by ensuring that the crop grows under optimal conditions and that pollination happens. Height is something every child who plants a sunflower wants for their plant, but for the sunflower farmer excessive height must be avoided if heavy rains and strong winds are not to knock the top-heavy plant over. Furthermore, sunflowers are cultivated in areas that are prone to various environmental

Anonymous Italian artist, *Sunflower*, 16th century.

Chrysanthemi Peruniani maximus flos.

stresses, including drought, waterlogging and high salinity, so the search is on for varieties that can thrive in such harsh conditions.

Wild sunflowers, like many Asteraceae, have mechanisms that prevent self-fertilization and promote pollination by insects. Insects, especially bees, are essential for seed to be set in wild sunflowers. Nectar is produced inside the bisexual disc florets, so to get at the energy-rich reward insects must push their mouthparts between the stamens and stigma, dusting their bodies with pollen and inadvertently transferring pollen between plants. Hybrid plants that make up the majority of commercial sunflower agriculture produce seed by self-pollination, so insects are irrelevant. However, insects are essential for producing industrial quantities of hybrid seed in the first place, since pollen must be transferred from male-fertile to male-sterile plants. Insects are vital environmental service providers, since without them the production of hybrid sunflower seed would be uneconomic. Breeders make sunflowers more enticing to insects by selecting for features that are attractive to pollinators, such as head colour, floret arrangement and form, and nectar composition.

Breeding new varieties of old crops requires enormous investment, in the same way that pharmaceutical companies must make huge investments to bring a new drug to market. Agricultural companies have therefore argued that they must recoup their costs, make a profit and protect their intellectual property.

The dramatic developments made in sunflower breeding over the last century show what we can achieve if suitable genetic variation is available. The conservation of genetic variation in sunflowers for future generations is therefore a pressing global responsibility. In the early twentieth century the Soviet geneticist Nikolai Vavilov became fascinated by crop variation. He was convinced that the greatest genetic variability occurred in the areas where the crop was first domesticated and where its close wild relatives were found. Vavilov and his students started to explore these regions of the world, collecting seeds and storing them in vast seed banks in the former Soviet

Ai Weiwei, *Sunflower Seeds*, October 2010, Turbine Hall, Tate Modern, London.

Union, such as that in Leningrad (St Petersburg).[23] Despite the efforts of those who looked after the collections, much of the genetic resource was lost after the Second World War and the collection had to be rebuilt.[24]

The storage of crop genes neither started nor ended with Vavilov and his colleagues. Today a worldwide network for the storage of both wild and domesticated plants exists, partly in the Svalbard Global Seed Vault, carved out of a mountain on this Norwegian island close to the North Pole.[25] The future of species in gene banks rests entirely with the managers and funders of such collections, the decisions they make and the information they have about the samples in their custody.

Managers of gene banks must combine global vision with conservatism: if a gene bank is to be useful, it must be actively managed.

Sustainable Harvest?

Modern human civilizations evolved after the last glaciation, during the 11,700-year-long Holocene epoch. The Industrial Revolution began in Britain about two hundred years ago and humans became major manipulators of global environmental processes, leading some people to call this the start of the Anthropocene epoch.[26] The Holocene's environmental limits with respect to processes such as changes in climate, biodiversity, land use and pollution must be a safe space for humans to survive. The Holocene therefore defines safe environmental boundaries for human life, allowing us to discover whether we have breached these boundaries during the early stages of the Anthropocene.

In the absence of a clear definition, 'sustainable' can become a 'weasel word' in the mouths of people and organizations exploiting, and protecting, environmental resources. During the enthusiastic lead-up to the United Nations Climate Change Conference in Copenhagen in 2009, in an attempt to focus attention on an objective measure of sustainability, an international group of researchers distilled many environmental features into a few variables, such as species extinction and pollution, and defined their planetary boundaries.[27]

The results of this audit were sobering. Agriculture is having negative environmental effects now, not in a remote future. Today, global species extinction and pollution levels, especially of nitrogen and phosphorus, are well beyond safe limits for humans, while the conversion of land from forest and climate change more broadly are moving beyond these limits.[28] Approaches to agriculture that reverse these trends must be found urgently if we are to avoid food production having additional long-term negative consequences for the planet.

Commercial plant breeding requires a market. One cannot assume that the same demands will always be present, as was seen with the drop in American sunflower production in the mid-1980s. New ways must therefore be found to manipulate old crops, and new crops must be investigated. Yet steps along these paths have provoked diverging opinions about plants' genetic resources and genetic modification, and raised concerns about the rights of peasant farmers as custodians of plant variation and plant genes as intellectual property.

Opening flower head of the central European thistle *Cirsium rivulare*, 'Atropurpureum'.

seven

Influencing

❀

Nemo me impune lacessit.

MOTTO OF THE STUART MONARCHS

The motto of the Stuart monarchs since the sixteenth century, 'no one attacks me with impunity', runs around the edge of one of the numerous types of pound coin that circulated in the United Kingdom until late 2017. The coin's reverse shows a thistle surrounded by a coronet. Thistles not only emblazon Scottish currency and royal and military heraldry, but are also used to market almost anything Scottish. Botanists have argued in vain which of the numerous thistles that grow in Scotland is the true Scottish thistle.[1] However, the botanical identity of the thistle is irrelevant; it has become a national symbol.

In the absence of evidence, explanations for the association have blossomed like thistles on wasteland and dispersed like thistledown on the wind. One explanation ascribes symbolism to the thistle's commonness, another links its biology with stereotypes of Scottish national characters: resilient, prickly, aggressive and tall. The most popular, and romantic, explanation is that when Vikings yelled out after stepping on sharp thistles during a night raid in 1263, the forces defending the Scottish shores were alerted and the invaders defeated.[2]

The power of flowers to become symbols has been used by political, religious and social leaders for centuries. The ultramarine-coloured crop-weed cornflower became a symbol of fertility and life in ancient

Cornflower with its prominent sterile flowers around the periphery of the flower head.

Egypt, before becoming associated with the Virgin Mary in Christian religious iconography.[3] However, plant symbols need not have ancient historic roots; they may be recent, since our cultural interaction with plants constantly changes.[4] For example, over the past century the poppy has become a powerful symbol of wartime tribute during British and Commonwealth Remembrance Day commemorations in November each year. The symbolism of the poppy can be traced to a poem written by John McCrae in 1915. In France, another weed that flourished in the devastation of the First World War battlefields, the cornflower (*bleuet de France*), symbolizes Armistice Day. When 298 people were killed in a plane crash in conflict-ridden eastern Ukraine in July 2014, both sides shifted blame as images of people's belongings scattered across fields of sunflowers were briefly flashed around the world. For one group of grieving Australian relatives, sunflower seed collected from these fields and raised in Australia became symbolic of grieving and remembrance.[5]

Language and Flowers

A few film-wrapped chrysanthemums purchased from a bucket in a petrol station are a cultural trope; a hastily considered, last-minute gift or peace offering. More poignantly, shrines of chrysanthemums left by roadsides may mark the sites of tragic accidents. Botanically, flowers are about sex, and the advertising industry would have us believe the same about human associations with flowers.[6] However, experimental evidence for the biological role of flowers and sex appeared only in 1694; the role of insects became understood much later.[7] Since most flowering plants were thought not to have sex, some Christian philosophers considered them pure; they had not been blemished by the Fall.[8] Flowers became symbols of purity, of courtly love, with meaning attached to form.

In Europe and the United States during the early nineteenth century, manuals began to appear formalizing literary codes, linking words with familiar flowers to create an intricate and nuanced 'language'.[9] Writers on the so-called language of flowers often cite the Turkish technique of unwritten communication, *salem*, as one of the language's roots, although *salem* is a mnemonic device rather than a way of attaching meaning to objects.[10] Other sources of pseudo-historical authority for attributing meanings to flowers include ancient civilizations, such as those of Egypt and China, and poetic works. Most egregious of all, some writers imply that meanings are somehow inherent in the 'character' of individual plants. Purveyors of the Doctrine of Signatures and astrological botany, who had tried to uncover plants' medicinal properties, had competition in the marketplace of mumbo-jumbo. Disputes among would-be botanical linguists, who showed 'more of ingenuity than wisdom', emerged as they promoted their books, jockeying for position in a highly competitive publishing

The common daisy, a ubiquitous part of lawns and playing fields in Britain.

market apparently aimed at women of a certain class.[11] In 1849 the 39-year-old printer and hymn writer Samuel Partridge differentiated his self-published work from competing titles by claiming divine authority: 'the fair daughters of the soul [plants] might reasonably be imagined to speak in a manner more improving and Christian.'[12]

Some flowers had the same meaning according to many authors, for example wormwood (absence) and yarrow (war).[13] There was no clear consensus on others, however; as with Lewis Carroll's Humpty Dumpty, words in the language of flowers meant whatever an author's flight of fancy might decide. One writer claimed that sunflower meant 'lofty and pure thoughts' and another 'false riches', while a third ascribed different meanings to short and tall sunflowers; ironically, in Partridge's Christian lexicon the sunflower denoted 'love of truth'.[14] In the case of burdock ('touch me not', importunity or rudeness) and dahlia ('for ever thine' or instability), contradictions were stark. As with manuals of manners, the right code book was necessary if social faux pas were to be avoided. Furthermore, givers and receivers of floriferous messages had to be passable taxonomists; confusing African (vulgar thoughts), French (jealousy) and garden (uneasiness) marigolds could be messy.[15] Idioms such as 'fresh as a daisy' fail to identify the specific daisy involved. Yet, in the confusion of languages with which flowers apparently speak, identity is important: daisy (innocence); garden daisy ('I share your sentiments'); wild daisy ('I will think of you'); and Michaelmas daisy (cheerfulness).[16] All plants in the nebulous category 'thistle' were considered evil. In the Japanese language of flowers (*Hanakotoba*), meanings are different yet again, for example daisy (faith) and dahlia (good taste).

Despite the number of books published on the language of flowers in the nineteenth century, and their popularity, these elaborate codes may not have been used beyond the confines of art and literature.[17] Pretentious specificities and imagined ancestry invite ridicule of the language of flowers, but flowers do have great symbolic value in our lives. Few occasions on the journey from the cradle to the grave are complete without floral tributes.

Other important links between culture, flowers and language are the names (vernacular or scientific) we give to Asteraceae, rather than the meanings we ascribe to them. Names, imposed by us, frequently tell us more about our preoccupations than about the plants. Common names, often steeped in belief systems and the environments in which people found themselves, could be essential survival tools, for instance by communicating whether a plant had toxic, culinary or medicinal properties.[18] Common names are constantly being invented, particularly for cultivars in the horticultural trade. Some names will become established, while others will fade away. Culture- and community-specific common names may retain elements of old languages, and may be remarkably stable across time; for example, the name 'groundsel' is derived from the seventh-century Anglo-Saxon name *gundesuilge* ('pus eater'), a reference to the plant's medicinal use.[19] Some plants generate many localized names; in Britain, for example, the common ragwort has been known by more than sixty names, including cankerweed, fairies' horse, fly flower, marefart, muggart and staggerwort.[20] As people emigrated they took the plants of their homelands, or their familiar names, to their adopted countries, perhaps christening unfamiliar plants with familiar names.

As British communities became more mobile, social pressure demanded the standardization or sanitization of names. In Britain, the scatological common names 'piss-a-bed' and 'shit-a-bed' were standardized to the more benign 'dandelion', although earthiness is retained in one of this plant's French common names, *pissenlit*.[21] However, attempts to standardize or proscribe common names risk the erosion of culturally specific information, the relegation of knowledge to elites with access to libraries and archives, or even the sanitization of awkward histories.

The etymological richness of common names is not lost in scientific names, which are no more complex than common names. Scientific names just happen to be written in a dead language that causes many people pronunciation problems: 'Dahlia was so named after Andreas Dahl, a Swede, and should be sounded Dar-le-a. Dalea [a legume], sounded as it is written, and named after our countryman [the apothecary Samuel] Dale, is quite a different plant.'[22] As with *Dahlia*, scientific names of plants in the sunflower family may commemorate great plant collectors, Asteraceae specialists or even scientists' patrons: *Barrosoa* after the Asteraceae specialist and *grande dame* of Brazilian botany Graziela Barroso; *Cassinia* after Henri de Cassini; *Eastwoodia* after the North American botanist and prolific collector Alice Eastwood; and *Lessingia* after the ill-fated Christian Lessing. Names may be derived from a plant's morphological or ecological features or its place of origin, for example *Osteospermum* ('bony seed'; a reference to the hard fruits), *abyssicolus* (inhabiting ravines or chasms) and *aegyptius* (from Egypt). Unsurprisingly, classical references abound in scientific names, such as *Anthemis*, *Arctium* and *Carduus*. More surprising may be the word games taxonomists play, as when Cassini, the great refiner of our understanding of the Asteraceae, discovered genera similar to Linnaeus' genus *Filago* and chose to name them using

Groundsel, one of the most common plants in the British Isles.

anagrams, including *Gifola*, *Logfia* and *Oglifa*. Linnaeus himself is known to have associated the characteristics of the plants he named with botanists' characters.[23] In the 1730s the Prussian botanist Johann Georg Siegesbeck became openly critical of the 'loathsome harlotry' of Linnaeus' Sexual System of plant classification.[24] Some have suggested that Linnaeus' naming of the weedy, smelly St Paul's wort in honour of Siegesbeck was a coded comment on his intellectual rival.

Over the last century, corporations and advertising agencies have exploited people's perceptions of flowers to associate themselves with vitality, wholesomeness, environmental purity and serenity. New floral symbols are constantly being created by advertisers; some will survive but others (perhaps most) will disappear. One that has stood the test of time is the edelweiss.

Edelweiss, Mountains and Tourists

The idea of edelweiss and the Alps is a cliché almost as strong as that associating thistles with the Scots. Edelweiss symbolism was deftly used in the Academy Award-winning film *The Sound of Music* (1969), a fictionalized interpretation of Maria von Trapp's memoir of events on the eve of the *Anschluss* in 1938. The film has become an anglophone Christmas ritual, and among its many well-known songs is the sentimental 'Edelweiss'. This song has become so familiar that some people believe it is an Austrian folksong or even the country's national anthem, rather than a tune and lyric written by the Americans Richard Rodgers and Oscar Hammerstein in the 1950s.[25]

Edelweiss is indeed an important part of the cultural heritage of people in the European Alps.[26] The vast majority of the thirty to forty species in the genus are not found in the Alps, but in the mountains of central and eastern Asia; only two species are European.[27] The commonest European species occurs at subalpine and alpine altitudes (2,000–3,000 m/6,500–10,000 ft) in the Pyrenees, Alps, Carpathians and Balkan Peninsula. Edelweiss is a short-lived plant that grows in open, nutrient-poor, close-cropped grasslands and is frequently found clinging to exposed, steep, often inaccessible, calcareous rock faces.[28] Some of these ecological features have contributed to edelweiss's strong, often romantic associations with the experience of visiting the Alps, images of health and purity, and dramatic feats:

> Much valued for the snowy purity of its colour, but still more so for the difficulty in getting it . . . [edelweiss] always grows on a spot to be reached only with the utmost peril . . . it is this very difficulty of acquisition which gives the flower so peculiar a value, and impels many a youth to brave the danger, that he may get a posy of Edelweiss for the hat or bosom of the girl he loves; and often has such a one fallen over the

Osteospermum, a cultivated Asteraceae.

rocks just as he had reached it, and been found dead; in his hand the flower of such fatal beauty, which he still held firmly grasped.[29]

In his mawkish nineteenth-century tale *Edelweiss* (1861), the German writer Berthold Auerbach summarized associations between edelweiss and the romance of alpine life: 'only the boldest alpine goatherds and hunters venture to pick the hardy little plant from its native soil. The possession of one is a proof of unusual daring.'[30] He went on to explain the plant as a memento, its appearance and name: 'a peculiar plant of delicate construction, and containing very little sap, so that it can be preserved a long while . . . The blossom is surrounded by

Edelweiss, a species that has come to symbolize the alpine regions of Europe over the last 200 years.

Edelweiss depicted on the obverse of the Austrian 1 Schilling coin, which was first minted in 1959 and was legal tender until 2001.

white velvety leaves, and even the stem has a down upon it . . . The Latin name is *Leontopodium alpinum*, which means Alpine lion's-foot.'

During the latter half of the eighteenth century, the Swiss geologist and physicist Horace-Bénédict de Saussure promoted the scientific exploration of the Alps, attracting people from outside the region to its beauty and drama. However, it was the publication of Karl Baedeker's handbook *Die Schweiz* (1844) and its English version, *Switzerland* (1863), that marked a turning point for tourism in the Alps. Weeks of arduous logistical preparation were no longer needed, while the railways made travel to luxurious hotels in alpine resorts simple. The edelweiss became symbolic of the healing power of fresh mountain air and unspoiled nature. Advertisers of the period began using all their wiles to ensure that edelweiss meant the Alps in the minds of their audience.[31]

Images of the edelweiss were spread on all manner of objects, and, importantly, on the novelty of the 1870s: postcards. Romantic stories of the dangers endured to win a few sprigs of edelweiss were spread, and visitors to the Alps returned home with their own, no doubt magnified, tales of daring. Such stories were scorned by seasoned alpinists such as the Englishman George Flemwell: 'The popular atmosphere surrounding this plant is charged with a goodly percentage of exaggeration. It is not rare for people fresh to Switzerland to pay her their first visit with brains obsessed by strange, weird myths and notions of Edelweiss.'[32] By the early twentieth century even some Swiss people expressed 'certain reservations with regard to this invasion of our mountains by the cosmopolitan crowd'.[33]

In addition to the apparent difficulty of seeing edelweiss, this plant had another feature that made it ideal for promoters of the alpine experience: dried specimens did not lose their colour. A scrap of dried edelweiss became an ideal physical memento of an alpine visit. The edelweiss trade began in earnest; fragments were stuck to postcards and bookmarks, and made into jewellery and pictures. The consequence was that edelweiss began to disappear from around the main tourist centres:

> Edelweiss was sold by the handful . . . guides, porters, and boys were tempted to rifle the mountain of its peerless flowers. When the rage for 'art greens' broke out in England, aesthetic young ladies crowned themselves with wreaths of these soft petals, or even appeared at fancy balls in the character of *The Alps*, smothered in edelweiss. At last the Swiss government determined to put down by law the wholesale destruction of this popular flower.[34]

But contempt comes on the tails of familiarity, as the once unfamiliar becomes commonplace. In his humorous account of a European tour, the American writer Mark Twain was not seduced by the myth of edelweiss during a visit to the Bernese Oberland in Switzerland:

> We did not find any example of the ugly Swiss favourite called Edelweiss. Its name seems to indicate that it is a noble flower and that it is white. It may be noble enough, but it is not attractive, and it is not white. The fuzzy blossom is the colour of bad cigar ashes, and appears to be made of a

cheap quality of gray plush. It has a noble and distant way of confining itself to the high altitudes, but that is probably on account of its looks . . . Everybody in the Alps wears a sprig of Edelweiss in his hat. It is the native's pet, and also the tourist's.[35]

Flemwell could hardly contain his scorn for the cult of the edelweiss, especially in comparison to alpine gentians: 'Perhaps it is not very venturesome to think that if the Edelweiss had become extinct, and were now to be found only amid the fastnesses of legend, it would live quite as securely in the hearts of men as it does at present; for its repute rests mostly upon the fabulous.'[36] Such criticism has not tarnished the 'image value' of the edelweiss; like the thistle in Scotland, edelweiss is used across the Alps.

Politics, Conservation and Commerce

The edelweiss has appeared on the currency and postage stamps of countries ranging from Switzerland and Austria through Romania to Kazakhstan. It is a heraldic element in the arms of towns and regions of alpine Europe, and has been adopted as an emblem by numerous alpine clubs and mountain-rescue services. Furthermore, the edelweiss is claimed as their national flower by at least two European countries: Austria and Switzerland. In *The Sound of Music*, the song 'Edelweiss' evoked Austrian nationalism. More than 25 years earlier, Herms Niel's march for Nazi Germany, 'Es war ein Edelweiss' (1941), had taken the association of dried edelweiss with memory and love, and combined it with sentiments of future happiness after the war: 'Und ich bin stolz darauf, denn diese zarte Blume schloß einst zwei Herzen auf' (And I am proud that this delicate flower joined our two hearts). In *Astérix chez les Helvètes* (Asterix in Switzerland; 1970), part of René Goscinny and Albert Uderzo's masterful series of parodies of national stereotypes, edelweiss became an essential ingredient in a miracle cure, and was firmly associated with Switzerland.

Selection of world postage stamps with members of the Asteraceae on them.

National flowers are tricky things. Scotland has her thistle and Japan her chrysanthemums, both strongly associated with their often legendary adoption by monarchs or emperors. However, neither symbol is as old as many people would like to believe. The chrysanthemum was introduced to Japan from China during the eighth century AD and became part of emperor Go-Toba's personal heraldry in the 1180s, but was adopted officially as part of the imperial seal (a stylized sixteen-rayed chrysanthemum) only in the 1880s.[37] The adoption of the dahlia as Mexico's national flower happened, by Presidential Decree, on 13 May 1963. The official reasons for its adoption were that most species are native to Mexico, one species commemorates a Mexican president and the genus has a history of pre-Hispanic cultivation.[38] It is perhaps chance that the date coincided with the opening of an exhibition of national floriculture. Other native Asteraceae adopted by nations include camomile by Russia and oxeye daisy by Latvia. The economic value of the non-native sunflower made it an obvious choice for Ukraine's national flower. Another non-native plant adopted as a national flower is Denmark's marguerite, a relative of the chrysanthemum endemic to the Canary Islands but long grown as a garden plant across Europe. Naturally, once flowers become national symbols they will be incorporated into military insignia, as edelweiss has been on the badges of central European countries with alpine regiments.

Since the nineteenth century the striking blue cornflower has been associated with countries as diverse as Belarus, Estonia and Germany, and, more recently, with Belarusian and Scandinavian political parties. Briefly, during the Austrian presidential election in 2016, much was made of the use of the cornflower by the nationalist Freiheitliche Partei

Chrysanthemum as depicted in a Japanese watercolour, dated 1700.

Österreichs (Freedom Party of Austria).[39] The short-lived Hungarian Revolution of 1918 adopted the aster as its symbol, while the edelweiss, allegedly Adolf Hitler's favourite flower, was adopted by the Edelweiß-piraten (Edelweiss Pirates), an anti-establishment German youth organization initially created in opposition to the regimentation of the Hitler Jugend.[40]

In a political cartoon of 1734, the sunflower symbolized the British prime minister, Robert Walpole.[41] By the start of the nineteenth

Range of knapweeds grown as annual plants in mid-Victorian British gardens.

century the sunflower was being used to caricature the City of London and its corruption under the Lord Mayor, Sir Charles Flower:

The Flow'r of the City, so gaudy and fine,
'Midst proud ones the proudest, was erst known to shine.
It spread its gay leaves and it shewed its rich clothes,
And to all (less in consequence) turn'd up its nose!
Till a blight, a sad blight, from a Democrat wind
Struck the Sensitive Plant both before and behind.
It felt the keen blast! All its arrogance fled,
And the Flow'r of the City hung, hung down its head.[42]

A few years later the sunflower was used to mock one incarnation of Napoleon Bonaparte: 'First as a Consular Toadstool, rising from a Corsican Dunghill, then changing to an Imperial Sun Flower, from that to an Elba Fungus and lastly to a bunch of Violets.'[43] During the Chinese Cultural Revolution (1966–76) propaganda posters depicted the Chinese people as sunflowers, surrounding and following the solar brilliance of Mao Zedong. The consequences and aftermath of this period in Chinese history are reflected on in the works of modern Chinese artists such as Ai Weiwei, in his installation sculpture *Sunflower Seeds* (2010), and Xu Jiang, in his depictions of drying and decaying sunflowers.

A major cultural and political development over the last forty years has been the recognition that human activities are having a detrimental effect on the planet. We have seen that as ideas of the fragility of the natural world were starting to be aired by a tiny minority of people at the end of the nineteenth century, measures were taken to protect edelweiss; perhaps more for the sake of the tourist industry than the plant itself.[44] Today edelweiss has protected status over much of its European range, and has come to represent the fragility of alpine environments. Other charismatic Asteraceae capable of representing vulnerable environments include the giant groundsels of East Africa, the frailejóns of the Andes and the silverswords of

Hawaii. At an altogether different scale, traditional meadows and grasslands around the world are often resplendent with colourful Asteraceae, for example oxeye daisies and hawkweeds in lowland European grasslands, tickseeds and blazing stars in the American prairies, and ligularias and senecios in high Chinese grasslands. Asteraceae in these habitats may be found nowhere else on the planet. They are apparently insignificant in their own right, but their brilliance en masse may give people pause for thought as they contemplate the destruction of these habitats and the pollinator services these areas provide for the production of our food.

As consumers have become concerned about the environments in which they live, corporations and companies have become interested

An earring made from a common daisy flower head embedded in plastic resin.

in aligning their images and products with such concerns. Images of women in soft-focus Asteraceae-filled meadows have been used to sell everything from chocolate bars and shampoos to sanitary products. An airline company uses dispersing dandelion fruits as a metaphor for freedom, while in advertiser's shorthand the daisy has taken on associations with innocence and purity. Images of real or imagined childhoods give daisies their power, and are summarized succinctly in Joyce Graham's hymn 'Daises Are Our Silver' (1931). In Charles Dickens's *David Copperfield* (1849–50), the worldly character James Steerforth nicknames the innocent eponymous hero 'Daisy'. Metaphors of childhood innocence were used starkly by Lyndon B. Johnson's campaign team in the presidential election of 1964 in the notorious 'Daisy' advertisement, in which a young girl playing with daisies was juxtaposed with images of nuclear holocaust.[45]

eight
Civilizing

❁

Stoop where thou wilt, thy careless hand
Some random bud will meet;
Thou canst not tread, but thou wilt find
The daisy at thy feet.
THOMAS HOOD (1799–1845), 'SONG'[1]

Unlike plant families such as the grasses, legumes or potatoes, the sunflower family produces few calorie bombs or medicines for humans. But it has contributed to our societies in other ways though: through cultural activities such as art, music, literature and science. The flamboyancy of Anthony van Dyck's attire in *Self-portrait with a Sunflower* (1632–3) matches the sunflower's brilliance. Paintings from Vincent van Gogh's *Sunflower* series (1888–9) have become cultural clichés, while 100 million handmade ceramic sunflower seeds in Ai Weiwei's *Sunflower Seeds* (2010) integrated the grand vision of an artist and the craftsmanship of the Chinese artisans who made these fruits. Still-life paintings from the Dutch Golden Age, subtly symbolizing the wealth and influence of their purchasers, abound with images of the natural world, including members of the sunflower family. In contrast, the exquisite detail of the backgrounds of tapestries, such as the early sixteenth-century series *Les Chasses de Maximilien*, exposes the splendour of commonplace, native European Asteraceae. At the level of the individual flower head, intersecting clockwise and anticlockwise

Sir Anthony van Dyck with a Sunflower (1644), etched by Wenceslaus Hollar, based on van Dyck's self-portrait.

spirals of florets reveal the beauty of mathematics and our interest in the mystical.

Whether we are 'hatching, matching or dispatching', Asteraceae are in the background and foreground of our cultural lives, for example daisies on nursery wallpapers, cornflowers in wedding bouquets and chrysanthemums at funerals. Familiar Asteraceae, with their distinctive flower heads, will naturally attract storytellers and songwriters, becoming woven into the myths and traditions that bind communities and peoples together. In southern Guangdong Province (China), the Xiaolan Chrysanthemum Festival has been held annually for more than eight hundred years, having survived the turmoil of imperial and revolutionary rule; across the East China Sea, Japanese chrysanthemum celebrations have also been held for centuries.[2] Outside eastern Asia, chrysanthemums appear in autumn flower shows, where gardeners engage in the serious business of showing off their horticultural prowess. The Burryman ritual involves a person clothed in burdock burrs being paraded through South Queensferry, near Edinburgh, on the second Friday of August each year.[3] The origin and meaning of the custom have been the subject of much speculation. There are records of the

One of Kazumasa Ogawa's many images of elaborate chrysanthemum cultivars grown in late 19th-century Japan.

Carline thistles,
Carlina vulgaris and
C. biebersteinii, whose
name reflects the
plants' mythological
associations
with Emperor
Charlemagne.

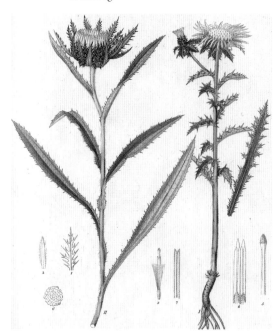

ritual from late seventeenth-century Scotland, although some argue
that it is far older; the Burryman may be a personification of the Green
Man, a scapegoat or even a lucky charm.

In the world's mythologies, it is virtually inevitable that gods
would transform demigods and mortals into Asteraceae, either in fits
of pique or magnanimity; in Romania, the maiden Florilor was transformed into a chicory plant to protect her from a spurned sun deity.[4]
Thistles are associated with Thor, the Nordic god of thunder, while
chicory reputedly transformed witches into rabbits and hares. Beyond
such old beliefs, marigolds and daisies have soteriological associations
with the Virgin Mary. Reminiscent of the thistle as *deus ex machina* in
Scottish legends, the carline thistle was supposedly revealed to the
emperor Charlemagne as a divine cure for plague, as he fought to unite
and Christianize eighth-century Western Europe; the myth is commemorated in the plant's scientific name, *Carlina*.[5] Naturally such rich
folklore encouraged people to incorporate these plants into their
cultural symbols.

Sunflowers are now part of global cultures, far removed from their origins on North American shores. They have become incorporated into paintings, literature and even songs. We have seen sunflowers as weapons in biting political satire and propaganda. The puppet 'Weed', widely thought to be a sunflower, became a popular character in the 1950s British children's television series *Bill and Ben*. Stylized sunflowers and other Asteraceae have been part of 'flower power' since the 1960s and '70s. In fewer than twenty human generations, New World sunflowers have been embraced by Old World cultures to become a global phenomenon.

Background and Foreground

Artists use plants in the background of their works to create impressions, enhance moods, convey particular meaning or merely brighten a dull environment. Frequently, the plants in such works are little more than vague forms. The Victorian designer William Morris and his imitators were inspired by the natural world to create elaborate wallpapers and textiles as part of the English Arts and Crafts Movement.[6] In the 1860s and '70s Morris's wallpapers included stylized designs inspired by daisies and sunflowers. The chrysanthemum has been a stylized element of Chinese painting since the tenth century. It is one of the Four Gentlemen, symbolic of nobility and the autumn, while in Japan it symbolizes the emperor, the imperial family and the Japanese nation.

Occasionally, one finds cases where background plants are treated with the same degree of skill as the main feature. Such an example is *The Hunt of the Unicorn* (1495–1505), a series of seven magnificent tapestries that interweave pre-Christian and Christian symbolism.[7] The tapestries were woven by craftsmen in Flanders from precious metals and wool and silk dyed with plant extracts. These artisans knew the natural world and filled the background of the tapestries with animals and plants. Ignoring ecological reality, spring- and summer-flowering woodland, grassland and mountain plants were mixed

Block-printed wallpaper with an Asteraceae design, manufactured by William Morris & Company, *c.* 1875.

together in an idyllic *millefleur* garden. Examples of Asteraceae in the tapestries include medieval favourites traditionally associated with the Virgin Mary, such as common and oxeye daisies and feverfew, and numerous sorts of thistles. Use of the orange-flowered marigold in the tapestry entitled *The Unicorn Dips His Horn into the Stream to Rid It of Poison* is obvious once one realizes that this plant was a universal theriac and an essential element of the medieval garden. Similar attention to detail is seen in the floral backgrounds of Islamic artworks, including sixteenth-century Persian carpets such as Ghyath ud-Din Jami's *Hunting Carpet* (1542–3). Albrecht Dürer's *Das große Rasenstück* (1503) revealed the beauty of yarrow leaves and developing heads of dandelion fruits in a sod of turf. Dürer's work emphasized botanical detail, in contrast to Claude Monet's borders of dahlias in *The Garden at Argenteuil* (1873) or Pierre-Auguste Renoir's *Chrysanthemums* (1881–2), which merely give an impression of the flowers they portray.

The heyday of botanical illustration came during the eighteenth and nineteenth centuries, but one of the earliest mentions of plant illustrations, other than for decorative or religious purposes, was by the first-century Roman writer Pliny the Elder. Pliny reported that illustrations were used as aids to plant identification, but he was critical:

> Not only is a picture misleading when the colours are so many, particularly as the aim is to copy Nature, but besides this, much imperfection arises from the manifold hazards in the accuracy of copyists. In addition, it is not enough for each plant to be painted at one period only of its life, since it alters its appearance with the fourfold changes of the year.[8]

By necessity, a botanical illustration, in whatever medium an artist chooses to use, thrusts the plant into the foreground. It is a detailed and scientifically accurate illustration, giving attention to features that distinguish one plant from another. Scientific botanical illustration requires attention to detail, accuracy and naturalism, based on detailed observation. Van Gogh's *Sunflower* series is aesthetically pleasing, but as scientific botanical illustrations his style is useless.

The alternative to an illustration for recording scientific information is a pressed, dried specimen. But 'plants preserved as dried herbarium specimens lose much that is essential to their character . . . and are thus of limited value as a currency for the exchange of botanical information.'[9] If this comment is to be believed, the resources that have gone into creating and maintaining collections of dried

The Unicorn in Captivity (1495–1505), one of the Unicorn Tapestries, showing a field of flowers including many different members of the sunflower family.

plants for more than four centuries have been wasted; their curators the 'sort of learned men, who are wholly employed in gathering together the refuse of nature'.[10] In fact, the specimen is the gold standard in botany, against which all else is judged. Whereas a botanical illustration relies on the abilities of the artist and a description on the language of the observer, the specimen has the characters that will allow objective confirmation of plant identification. In reality, illustrations, descriptions and specimens complement one another.

In the last decades of her life, the eighteenth-century intellectual Mary Delany, a close friend of Margaret Bentinck, Dowager Duchess of Portland, made curious – and beautiful – simulacra of herbarium specimens. Mrs Delany made more than 1,000 botanical 'mosaicks', including many Asteraceae.[11] The two women shared a deep interest in plants, and the Duchess had the fortune necessary to indulge that interest as she created the largest natural history collection in eighteenth-century Britain.[12] Delany wrote that 'the paper mosaic work was begun in the seventy-fourth year of my age . . . I should have dropped the attempt as vain had not the Duchess Dowager of Portland looked on it with favourable eyes.'[13] Delany's method was described by her biographer:

> Mrs. Delany placed the growing plant before her. Behind it she put a sheet of black paper . . . She did not draw the plant, but by her eye cut out each flower, or rather each petal, as it appeared; the lights and shades were afterwards cut out, and laid on, being pasted one over the other. The stamina and leaves were done in the same manner, in various coloured papers . . . that part of the work which appears likely ever to remain a mystery is the way in which by the eye alone scissors could be directed to cut out the innumerable parts necessary to complete the outline and shading . . . as if they had been produced instantaneously by the stroke of a magic wand.[14]

The collages Delany made are mounted on black paper and have the layout of herbarium specimens, but are coloured as in life. During her lifetime, her creations were praised by her contemporaries, including the artist Joshua Reynolds and the artist-politician Horace Walpole. Charles Darwin's grandfather Erasmus fawned over the work, although from his descriptions it is clear that he had never seen it.[15] Joseph Banks, the most prominent botanist of late eighteenth-century Britain, also flattered: 'Her paper representations of flowers were the only imitations of Nature he had ever seen from which he could venture to describe botanically any plant without the least fear of making a mistake.'[16]

For a botanical illustration to be of greatest scientific value, it must be 'worth 10,000 words'. No matter how aesthetically pleasing and well executed a botanical illustration might be, if it does not illustrate a plant's features accurately its scientific role has failed. The nineteenth-century artist and critic John Ruskin made the case for the importance of botanical illustration: 'It is difficult to give [plants] the accuracy of attention necessary to see their beauty without drawing them.'[17]

Herbals contain the names and descriptions of herbs, or plants in general, with their properties and uses. Some of the earliest illustrated herbals exist only as manuscripts, for example the 'Vienna Dioscorides', an early sixth-century AD illuminated manuscript of Dioscorides' *De Materia medica*.[18] More than 1,500 years of slavish copying of Dioscorides' illustrations, whether in scriptoria or using William Caxton's revolutionary printing press, rendered many of the illustrations unrecognizable.

In terms of botanical illustration, the age of modern botany came in 1530 with the publication of Otto Brunfels's *Herbarum vivae eicones* (Living Pictures of Herbs). While the text was second-rate and typical of the botany of the time, Hans Weiditz's naturalistic woodcut illustrations were a revelation. Brunfels clearly never studied the plants he mentioned in the field, and indeed appeared not to realize that floras vary from region to region. In contrast, Weiditz knew plants in the

Chinese aster, a hand-coloured copper engraving, made by the botanist Johann
Dillenius for his book of rare horticultural novelties, *Hortus Elthamensis* (1732).

Adriaen van Utrecht, *Still Life with Game, Vegetables, Fruit and a Cockatoo*, 1650, oil on canvas, including a bunch of globe artichokes.

field, and presented them in a way that might be mistaken for the work of Dürer, under whom he studied. However, in Hieronymus Bock's *New Kreutterbuch* (1539) the author had made direct observations of plants. Leonhart Fuchs merged the advantages of Brunfels's and Bock's works to produce a masterpiece, *De Historia stirpium* (On the History of Plants; 1542), a catalogue of about five hundred plants growing in Germany. Fuchs's illustrations, often using the actual woodblocks from the earlier works, were reproduced across Europe until the end of the eighteenth century. These works went on to inspire designers of the nineteenth-century Pre-Raphaelite and Arts and Crafts movements, and early twentieth-century Art Nouveau.

Concerns over using plant illustrations as evidence may appear to be abstruse, yet illustrations may be the only evidence we have about the history of familiar Asteraceae. The dahlia, a commonplace garden plant of late summer in Europe, originated in Mexico.[19] The plant's earliest mention appears to be in the *Codex Badianus* or *Libellus de Medicinalibus Indorum Herbis*, the first illustrated botanical text written in the post-Columbian Americas. The *Codex* is a Latin translation of an Aztec botanical and medicinal text, including plants of Aztec gardens, written by the Christianized Aztec Martín de la Cruz in 1552. The images, however, are highly stylized; they can be interpreted as various different members of the sunflower family. Not only does this document

Karl Blossfeldt,
Serratula Nudicaulis
(*Sawwort*), 1928.

provide historical evidence for the dahlia's Mexican origin, but also it has, by stretching the limits of the evidence, been used to assert that the dahlia was Montezuma's favourite flower: gold dust for advertisers. In another empire, on another continent, Napoleon's consort, the empress Josephine, apparently became protective over at least one botanical prize in her garden at the Château de Malmaison, Paris: her dahlias, leading to claims that this was her favourite flower. Yet, looking at the work of Pierre-Joseph Redouté, the botanical artist most closely associated with the empress's garden, one must conclude that roses had a greater claim to her affections.[20]

That the primarily artistic can have scientific value is seen in the outstanding close-up black-and-white photographic studies of plants made by the German artist and teacher Karl Blossfeldt. These photographs were conceived as teaching aids and, beyond his students, Blossfeldt's work was unknown until shortly before his death in

1932. The publication of *Urformen der Kunst* (Art Forms in Nature; 1928) revealed the precision and beauty of his work, and inspired generations of both scientific and artistic photographers.

Spirals and Symmetry

Naturalistic and impressionistic interpretations of Asteraceae are used in apparently endless ways to decorate all manner of objects, from pottery and porcelain through jewellery and book jackets to plastic toys and paper bags. Cornflowers and thistles appear in designs as diverse as Iznik ceramics from the mid-sixteenth century to twentieth-century American Stangl pottery or Corning and Pilkington glassware. Popular designs tend to concentrate on a limited range of the vast diversity of Asteraceae. Designers are probably attracted to the family by the flowers' bold colours and forms, and their symmetry – precisely the qualities Blossfeldt's photographs revealed.

In the late eighteenth century the German poet and philosopher Johann Wolfgang von Goethe became fascinated by the form and the apparent similarity of organs within plants. In 1790 he published his conclusions in his first major botanical work, *Versuch die Metamorphose der Pflanzen zu erklären* (The Metamorphosis of Plants). He argued that

Ceramics with Asteraceae motifs: 1950s Stanglware with thistle design from the USA and a modern mug decorated with a 19th-century image of Oxford ragwort.

Floret packing in the Asteraceae flower head; 13 anticlockwise spirals and 21 clockwise spirals are marked; 50, 250 and 1,000 florets are shown in the central column. The bottom row shows the effects of varying the angle of separation of adjacent florets: 137.68, 137.50 and 137.34 degrees.

leaf-like structures showed a transformation from seed leaves, through true leaves to petals and other flower parts.[21] Goethe's work was a major development in our understanding of plant form, presaging major developments in evolutionary biology from the mid-nineteenth century to the present day.[22] One familiar pattern he spotted was the spiral. In terms of Goethe's ideas, the sunflower becomes spirals of leaves giving way to spirals of bracts surrounding the flower head and spirals of florets in the flower head.

Intersecting spirals are seen in the flower heads of many Asteraceae, although as the flower heads get smaller the pattern becomes less obvious. Although Goethe had spotted the pattern, as had eighteenth-century natural philosophers, it required the skill of the French physicists Auguste and Louis Bravais to describe the geometry. The brothers found that leaves and florets, indeed many organs in the natural world, were separated by an angle of 137.5 degrees – 'the golden angle'.[23] The explanation of how geometry related to plant growth required more than a century of additional scientific research.

Spirals, or the illusion of spirals, are found throughout nature.[24] Many have a specific mathematical relationship at their heart: the Fibonacci series – 0, 1, 1, 2, 3, 5, 8, 13, 21 and so on. The series is named after a thirteenth-century Italian mathematician, Leonardo of Pisa, although it was known to ancient Indian mathematicians. In it, each number is the sum of the two previous numbers.

Furthermore, dividing one number by the subsequent number produces another number series: 1, 0.5, 0.666 . . . 0.6, 0.625, 0.615 . . ., whose values converge on an irrational number known as phi (φ) (the best-known irrational number is pi, π). In popular culture, phi is known as the 'golden number', 'golden ratio' or 'golden mean'. When people searched for the number in many parts of the fabricated and natural world they found it, frequently leading to spurious mystical conclusions about its significance.[25]

The two spirals (clockwise and anticlockwise) seen in large sunflower heads are associated with our perception of plant growth. Sunflowers, like all plants, grow from shoot tips. Around these tips are tiny lumps of cells (primordia) jostling for optimal space (137.5 degrees apart); the primordia eventually develop into structures such as leaves, bracts and flowers. As the tip grows the primordia are left behind, so the oldest primordia are furthest away from the growing tip. The tightly wound spiral produced by the order of primordia development is the generative spiral. In contrast, the spirals we see in sunflower heads are from neighbouring primordia. The slightest change in the angle of the generative spiral destroys the uniformity of the pattern and the packing of the florets.[26]

It is frequently assumed that the numbers of clockwise and anticlockwise spirals in sunflower heads are adjacent Fibonacci numbers (such as 55 and 89). Gathering the information to test this hypothesis formally requires a large number of observations, using rigorous protocols. Citizen science, a twenty-first-century term for a centuries-old practice, has emerged as an approach by which people, most of them not formally trained as scientists, are encouraged to gather scientific data. Benefits to both professional and citizen scientists emerge when volunteers collecting large volumes of data become involved in the scientific process, and when academics communicate their research to diverse audiences. A citizen-science investigation of UK-grown sunflower heads showed that Fibonacci structures were the most frequent arrangement of spirals observed.[27] However, there were many examples of more complex non-Fibonacci structures.

Clearly variation – the raw material of evolution – occurs in the number of clockwise and anticlockwise spirals of a sunflower head.

In Words and Music

In nineteenth-century England, the 'Village Minstrel', John Clare, described daisies as 'decking the green', as 'silver studs' and 'gemmed in dew'; a familiar background to our lives.[28] The daisy has been used by English writers since at least the fourteenth century. Geoffrey Chaucer described the common daisy as 'the emperice, and floure of floures alle', and they were used to decorate the margins of fifteenth-century manuscripts showing lovers meeting on daisy-speckled lawns in enclosed gardens.[29] William Shakespeare uses daisy imagery to describe his heroine in the *Rape of Lucrece* (1594): 'Without the bed her other fair hand was,/ On the green coverlet; whose perfect white/ Show'd like an April daisy on the grass.' In 'To a Mountain Daisy (On Turning One Down with the Plough in April 1786)', the Scottish poet and ploughman Robert Burns reflected on the daisy's fate and the brevity of our lives: 'Ev'n thou who mourn'st the Daisy's fate,/ That fate is thine – no distant date;/ Stern Ruin's plough-share drives, elate,/ Full on thy bloom,/ Till crush'd beneath the furrow's weight,/ Shall be thy doom!' A similar sentiment is expressed in the English euphemism 'pushing up the daisies'; in France, the reference is to dandelions (*manger les pissenlits par la racine*).

Alice's contemplation of 'whether the pleasure of making a daisy-chain would be worth the trouble of getting up and picking the daisies' began one of the best-known stories in children's literature, Lewis Carroll's *Alice's Adventures in Wonderland* (1865). Part of the appeal of such simple garlands, which become crowns and tiaras, bracelets and belts in a child's imagination, lies in their 'head-to-tail' repetition and symmetry of form. Repetition and symmetry make daisy-chain analogies commonplace in fields as diverse as computing, mathematics, crochet, transplant surgery, angling and molecular biology. Daisies also take pride of place in the romantic mantra 'He loves me, he loves

Page from the manuscript of *Chroniques*, Book Three, *c.* 1480, showing a margin decorated with plants such as thistles and strawberries.

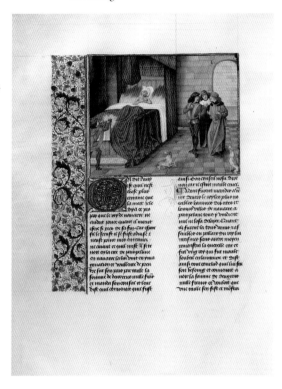

me not'; if love is desired, be sure to pick an odd-rayed flower head. However, the most famous daisies in English literature are probably the ambiguous heroine of Henry James's *Daisy Miller* (1879) and the self-absorbed Daisy Buchanan of F. Scott Fitzgerald's *The Great Gatsby* (1925).

Another famous Daisy appears in Harry Dacre's 'Daisy Bell' ('Bicycle Built for Two'; 1892).[30] Besides its popularity as a music-hall standard, the song went on to become a footnote in computing history when IBM used it to demonstrate artificial speech synthesis in 1961; that was later picked up by Arthur C. Clarke in *2001: A Space Odyssey* (1968). More momentous events are commemorated in a song lyric by the American folk-rock group The Decemberists. 'When the War Came' (2006), with surely the only lyric ever to combine the name of the Soviet geneticist Nikolai Vavilov and the word 'Asteraceae', commemorates the self-sacrifice of the stewards of the city's seed

Floral mutant of the common daisy, which is often cultivated as a garden plant.

collection during the Siege of Leningrad: they starved rather than eat the contents of the collection.[31]

The symbolism of the Asteraceae in modern popular culture continues to evolve as their images have been adopted as emoticons by social media, and people continue to invest meanings in these plants. However, it is in the world's garden and flower markets that the Asteraceae have been a consistent, influential presence for hundreds of years.

nine
Cultivating

✿

Not only is the science of horticulture now studied with a view to the attainment or aggrandisement of pecuniary wealth . . . for the retired tradesman and gentleman to the most influential nobleman, and even with ladies of the highest rank and first distinction, this study has now become a favourite pursuit.

JOSEPH PAXTON, *A Practical Treatise on the Cultivation of the Dahlia* (1838)[1]

Asteraceae, the weeds of the world, come together in our gardens; some we nurture and cosset until they become a problem, others we despise and try to exterminate. After centuries of painting our gardens and homes with Asteraceae, one might have thought the horticulturalist's palette of colour and form was vast enough to satisfy even the most fervid imagination. Yet breeders are constantly producing new sorts: a modification of petal shape here, a slight change of hue there, and, of course, the constant battle to ensure that plants are resistant to pathogens. In the seventeenth century florists – the breeders of garden plants and the geneticists of their day – revelled in the range of variation within a species, and what could be achieved by the simple act of selective breeding.[2] However, their activities were derided by serious botanists such as Carolus Linnaeus, who warned that 'these men cultivate a science peculiar to themselves, the mysteries of which are known only to the

adepts; nor can such knowledge be worth the attention of the botanist; wherefore let no sound botanist ever enter into their societies.'[3]

European gardens are replete with cultivated Asteraceae, and the products of breeders' skill; more than eight hundred species, from 190 genera, are commonly grown.[4] P. G. Wodehouse's alphabetical litany of blooms under the protection of Angus McAllister at Blandings Castle (recited in *Lord Emsworth and the Girl Friend*, 1935) can readily be recomposed solely of Asteraceae: *Achillea*; *Bellis*; *Chrysanthemum*; *Dahlia*;

Rough hawksbeard, a native of western and central Europe, is found as a casual plant of waste places.

Echinops; Felicia; Gerbera; Helianthus; Inula; Jurinia; Kleinia; Liatris; Marshallia; Notobasis; Olearia; Pulicaria; Rudbeckia; Solidago; Tagetes; Urospermum; Verbesina; Wedelia; Xeranthemum; and *Zinnia.*

In addition to their diversity in our gardens, a handful of Asteraceae – among them asters, chrysanthemums, dahlias and gerberas – are important contributors to the commercially valuable cut-flower

Perennial border in Oxford Botanic Garden containing numerous autumn-flowering Asteraceae.

trade; in 2015 the global trade was worth nearly U.S.$8.5 billion. The Netherlands and Columbia accounted for 62 per cent of all exports, while the United States and Germany were responsible for nearly a third of all cut-flower imports.[5] This vast floral trade is also associated with environmental problems such as water pollution, and with social problems such as exploitation and economic dependency.[6]

Asters, chrysanthemums and dahlias have attracted growers for centuries, and societies devoted to their appreciation have been formed worldwide. Thousands of different cultivars have been bred for pleasure or profit; fewer than 150 years after the introduction of the dahlia to Europe and North America, 14,000 different cultivars were recorded.[7] However, fondness for Asteraceae is not restricted to North Americans and Europeans. Chinese and Japanese gardeners took the art of chrysanthemum culture to great heights millennia before the plants were even seen by Europeans, while the Ottomans, together with their weakness for tulips, were fascinated by knapweeds.[8] In medieval European gardens, ornamental Asteraceae jostled for space with more utilitarian species.[9]

Coaxing plants to grow under artificial conditions can be difficult, and is a luxury for the few who have the time and money to experiment. Yet ornamental plants also attract the many: 'so high do these plants [chrysanthemums] stand in the favour of the Chinese gardener, that he will cultivate them extensively, even against the wishes of his employer; and, in many instances, rather leave his situation than give up the growth of his favourite flower.'[10] Just as war spurs technological development, so competition and one-upmanship among gardeners enhance the diversity of plants grown in gardens.

For a wild plant to be introduced successfully into horticulture, its nature (genetics) and nurture (environment) must be right. Plants reach the peak of their genetic potential when they are grown in optimal conditions. However, these conditions may be markedly different from those found in natural habitats. In August 2014 a German-grown sunflower was coaxed to a height of 9.17 m (just over 30 ft), but to achieve this it was necessary to have the right genetic material combined with the grower's care.[11]

New Homes

Getting a seed or growing plant to its new home is not enough if it is to be exploited; the plant must thrive and survive. It is no surprise, therefore, that the exotics that are easiest to grow are capable of flourishing with little help from their new masters. Many popular

Mixed border of annual plants including marigolds, cornflower and tickseed.

plants that have been successfully cultivated are highly adaptable and capable of rapid growth under a wide range of conditions. These features describe both an ideal cultivated plant and a region's weeds. Many familiar Asteraceae are easily grown survivors that are difficult to kill, for example common daisies and North American asters. However, other introduced species are much more difficult to grow, and require all the ingenuity and experience of generations of gardeners.[12]

The acquisitive botanist and gardener wants to have what his or her rivals have acquired, and be surrounded by his or her own novelties. Other, less mercenary motivations to cultivate new plants may include the wish to ensure that desirable plants are not lost. Many cultivated plants are killed by disease, lack of interest or changing fashion. The obsession of one generation may readily be cast aside by the next; gardening books from the last century are filled with lists of plants that are not cultivated in the present one. If the evidence of a plant's cultivation is not to be confined to books or herbaria, botanical insurance is needed to ensure that living plants survive; plants must be propagated.

Two basic approaches to propagation can be employed: sexual propagation from seed and clonal propagation from cuttings. Seeds are mobile, self-contained, desiccation-tolerant packets that germinate in response to environmental conditions. They are the obvious means of moving plants from their natural homes into gardens. Furthermore, if plants produce abundant, fertile seed in cultivation, that seed can be readily dispersed by sale or exchange. Seed exchange was practised for millennia within and among communities as an activity associated with the annual cycles of food production. Yet seed does not live forever; it loses viability over time. The viability of seed depends on the species, and ranges from a matter of weeks to tens of years. Until the advent of storage facilities that could be kept cold and dry, seeds needed to be grown regularly to maintain fresh supplies.

Dormancy is a natural survival characteristic of most seeds and may take numerous forms. However, once the seed starts to germinate, there is no going back. A seedling must cope with whatever conditions surround it, or it will die. Without understanding the basis of seed dormancy, gardeners have been very effective at overcoming it. In some cases merely storing seed is sufficient; in others it is necessary to damage the seed, chill it or even expose it to smoke.

Clonal propagation relies on the fact that any living plant cell can regenerate into any other plant cell, a condition called totipotency. Anyone who has broken a leaf or stem from a desired plant, pushed it into soil and seen it transform into a new plant is familiar with the process. Totipotency has been the basis of plant theft and propagation technology for millennia. Trial and error by generations of gardeners have meant that much horticultural wisdom, and mythology, has developed around which parts of a plant are most appropriate for propagation in which species. Simply splitting large plants or snapping off runners and offsets are effective means of propagating North American asters. The Scottish plant collector Robert Fortune took cuttings from chrysanthemums in Japanese gardens in the 1860s, leading to the transformation of Western chrysanthemums.[13] Fortune was greatly aided in his efforts by Nathaniel Ward's invention of an enclosed,

Kazumasa Ogawa's chrysanthemum garden (1896) showing the care given to chrysanthemum culture in late 19th-century Japan.

184

Variation in Chinese asters grown as annual plants in mid-Victorian British gardens.

glazed box (the Wardian Case), which protected growing plants from the elements on board ship.[14]

Getting the Right Genes

Most Asteraceae are exotic to the places where they are currently bred, tended and traded. Growers of chrysanthemums and dahlias, even two hundred years ago, would hardly recognize the plants that are cultivated today. The chrysanthemum grown for thousands of years in China became known in the West only in the late seventeenth century, and a few desultory attempts were made to grow it in the early eighteenth century.[15] Serious European interest in chrysanthemums had to wait until 1789, when a Marseilles businessman, Pierre-Louis Blancard, imported a large-flowered purple variety from China. A year later it reached British shores, and it was eventually illustrated in the press with the cautious comment that the chrysanthemum 'promises to become an acquisition highly valuable'.[16]

In subsequent years additional breeding material was acquired from China, adding new colours and forms to the chrysanthemum flower head. In Britain, by 1826 the Horticultural Society could boast 48 varieties in its gardens.[17] All were raised from cuttings; seeds would not ripen in cold European winters. By the end of the 1820s chrysanthemums had been raised from seedlings, revealing tremendous new variation to delight breeders' eyes. In 1840 the English chrysanthemum enthusiast John Salter had three to four hundred varieties of chrysanthemum in his nursery at Versailles.

Salter credited the Chinese with generating 'the first sports or rude varieties', which were perfected in Europe; 'the Chrysanthemum of China was . . . almost useless as compared with the Chrysanthemum which is now the most beautiful ornament of our winter gardens.'[18] He was aware of only the tip of a Chinese diversity iceberg, since in 1630 more than five hundred cultivars had been recorded in China.[19] During the 1840s Robert Fortune was exploring China, often covertly, for choice new plants that would grow in Britain.[20] Among his many introductions that transformed our gardens were two small-flowered chrysanthemums. These were too small for British taste, but the French were delighted by them and eventually bred pompon-type chrysanthemums from them. Fortune's contribution to the history of the chrysanthemum was not over, however, and during a visit to Japan in the 1860s he

Qing dynasty Chinese jade dish in the shape of a chrysanthemum flower, from the 18th or 19th century.

procured some extraordinary varieties, most peculiar in form and in colouring, and quite distinct from any of the kinds at present known in Europe. One had petals like long thick hairs, of a red colour, but tipped with yellow, looking like the fringe of a shawl or curtain; another had broad white petals striped with red like a carnation or camellia; while others were remarkable for their great size and brilliant colouring. If I can succeed in introducing these varieties into Europe, they may create as great a change amongst chrysanthemums as my old protegee the modest 'Chusan daisy' did when she became the parent of the present race of pompones.[21]

Today there are thousands of different forms of chrysanthemum artificially selected from crosses among genetic lineages introduced from China and Japan. These forms are now grouped into thirteen classes ranging from simple single and semi-doubles through decoratives, incurves and pompons to more exotic-sounding classes such as anemones, spoons, quills and spiders. Even before the chrysanthemum left China for Japanese shores in the eighth century AD, it was probably a complex interspecific hybrid; that genetic complexity has only increased over the last century.

One Asteraceae that has regained its popularity since the 1960s is the cultivated gerbera. These are artificial hybrids between the Transvaal daisy, a species endemic to parts of the African Transvaal and Swaziland, and *Gerbera viridifolia*, which is distributed through eastern Africa.[22] In modern cultivated gerberas, the genetic material

Transvaal daisy, one of the parents of the popular and economically important cut flower gerbera.

was taken from wild African material collected in the late nineteenth century. The Transvaal daisy was discovered in the 1870s but was not introduced to Britain until more than a decade later. The director of the Royal Botanic Garden at Kew, Joseph Hooker, recognized the plant's horticultural potential but seemed rather disappointed when he wrote that 'the colour of the rays must be much brighter in its native country than here, for that gentleman [Harry Bolus, who first described the plant] describes them as flame-coloured.'[23] By the end of the nineteenth century much breeding, hybridization and selection had been undertaken by Richard Lynch at the Cambridge Botanic Garden.[24] However, public interest in the gerbera declined and it was not until after the Second World War that it was reignited. The result is a vast range of flower-head form and hue, often in bold colours, that makes gerberas one of the world's most important cut flowers.[25]

The right genes, in the right plants and in the right place, have enormous economic value. The golden age of plant collecting in the nineteenth century, and the establishment and expansion of the botanic gardens by European colonial powers, was driven by the economic value of the genetic exploitation of plants.[26] In 1851 spectacular displays of agricultural, horticultural and other economic plants at the Great Exhibition in London showed people just how valuable the natural world could be. Today plant exploitation is wrapped up in concepts of natural capital and the provision of environmental services, such as pollination for crops and the protection of water resources.

Catering for the Masses

Once the right genetic types are in cultivation, additional manipulations of a species' growing environment may be necessary to ensure that it performs at its best, when we want it to do so. As we have seen, chrysanthemums come in a wide range of colours, shapes and sizes. Some of these grow well outside and are the familiar autumn chrysanthemums; others have been manipulated to grow indoors. Two common manipulations of chrysanthemums are the removal of lateral

A cultivar of the horticultural cineraria, a hybrid species of the Macaranesia genus *Pericallis*.

buds to change the form and the manipulation of photoperiod to change the flowering time.

Plant stems have two types of bud: terminal buds and lateral buds, both of which may become stems or flowers. Terminal buds generally dominate over lateral buds; if terminal buds are removed, lateral buds take over. Such responses have been used by gardeners for centuries to manipulate form, for example when clipping hedges. In standard chrysanthemums, all lateral buds are removed from single-stemmed plants to leave a large terminal flower head. Typical pot chrysanthemums are produced from multi-stemmed plants where all the lateral buds have been removed from each stem. Spray chrysanthemums have the terminal bud removed so that lateral flower heads develop.

Robert Fortune encountered such chrysanthemum topiary and manipulation in nineteenth-century China:

> There is no other plant with which he [the Chinese] takes so much pains, or which he cultivates so well . . . he stands unrivalled. The plants themselves seem, as it were, to meet him half way and grow just as he pleases; sometimes I found them trained in the form of animals, such as horses and deer, and at other times they were made to resemble the pagodas, so common in the country. Whether they were trained into these fanciful forms, or merely grown as simple bushes, they were always in high health . . . About Shanghae and Ning-po the chrysanthemum is still better managed than it is near Canton . . . The Chinese are fond of having very large blooms, and, in order to obtain these, they generally pick off all the small flower-buds.[27]

In the mid-twentieth century, academic research into the manipulation of photoperiod had a critical impact on the profitability of cultivating chrysanthemums. Photoperiod is the change in the length of the daily dark period, which sets off flower development in some plants. Plants were divided into three broad groups, named when the relative importance of light and dark was not fully understood: long-day, short-day and day-neutral. Long-day plants require a short period of darkness to signal a change, while a short-day plant requires a long night to elicit a change. The many plants that show no response to light are described as day-neutral. The chrysanthemum is a short-day plant; when days are shorter than a certain critical period, it will produce flowers, and when the days are longer than the critical period it will produce leaves. Furthermore, chrysanthemums are known to have two critical periods, one for giving rise to flowers and the other for developing them. Both periods vary according to temperature and cultivar. Before these discoveries, chrysanthemums were a seasonal crop of temperate regions, grown during a short period in autumn

Pub by W. Curtis S.ᵗ Geo: Crescent Feb.1.1796

Chrysanthemum indicum was introduced to Britain as an ornamental as early as 1795.

to take advantage of natural rapid changes in day length. Today, day length, temperature and cultivar can be manipulated to supply the global, year-round demand for chrysanthemums.

Plants that were once seasonal have become commonplace all year round. It is now possible to have the displays of chrysanthemums that Fortune witnessed in Japan, all year long:

> The most curious objects in this garden were imitation ladies made up out of the flowers of the chrysanthemum. Thousands of flowers were used for this purpose; and as these artificial beauties smiled upon the visitors out of the little alcoves and summer houses, the effect was oftentimes rather startling.[28]

The vast majority of Asteraceae selected by breeders have a very short half-life in commercial markets. Only those that can be maintained in the face of disease and that appeal to the mass market will survive. Those that do survive in cultivation may tell us something about what people care about, what they are willing to buy and perhaps what they want to pass on to future generations.

Changing the Asteraceae Capitulum

Collectors and growers of sunflowers are aware of how dramatically the form and colour of sunflower heads differ from the stereotype.[29] Van Gogh's *Sunflower* series of paintings shows numerous ways in which the sunflower head varies. Ray florets range from red to deep orange through golden yellow to pale yellow and cream, while disc florets can become very deep purple. In form, ray florets may become tubular, while disc florets may become similar in appearance to ray florets. Such variation is not restricted to cultivated Asteraceae. For example, in the Oxford Physic Garden in the latter half of the seventeenth century, there were feverfew mutants that the first keepers of the Garden had collected from wild populations: 'simplici', the common type, had white ray florets and yellow disc florets; 'bullatis floribus' had only disc florets; 'fistuloso' had tubular ray florets; and 'flore pleno' had disc florets similar to ray florets.[30] In the hands of plant breeders, natural variation in floral form and colour has been selected to create enormous numbers of cultivars in horticultural plants such as chrysanthemums, dahlias, gerberas and daisies.

Variation is the product of mutation, a natural process whereby DNA is permanently changed. In popular culture, mutants bring images of monsters to mind. Yet mutants are the raw material of evolution and the horticultural industry, where they are often called 'sports'. The most frequent variant in a natural population is called the wild type. In addition to natural mutants, breeders also have artificial mutants, produced by exposure to radiation, such as X-rays, gamma rays or ultraviolet light, or chemicals. The vast majority of mutations are lethal or have no effect on a plant's appearance. Since mutation is random, sports will occasionally be thrown up with commercial value that can be either exploited directly or crossed into existing cultivars.

Biological reasons for variation in flower colour, such as attracting pollinators, have been taken over by humans to become things of beauty. Hundreds of garden dahlia cultivars have been named based on the colour of the flower head. In the case of the garden dahlia, three classes of pigment are responsible for the spectrum of colours. Anthrocyanins produce magenta, purple, crimson and scarlet, chalcones and aurones produce yellows, and flavones and flavanones produce ivory pigments.[31] These pigments are produced by complex biochemical pathways, where enzymes control each step from one chemical to another. The instructions for building each enzyme are genes in the DNA. If a gene is mutated, an enzyme may not be produced or its activity may be modified, leading to changes in the production of pigment and hence flower colour. Other factors, such as the number of copies of a particular gene, may also influence the colour of the flower. We know that only a few genes are responsible for the vast array of colour variation found in the dahlia, but they interact in intricate fashions. Given such complexities, unpicking the

Garden zinnias.

inheritance of dahlia colour was a surprising success for the science of genetics in its twentieth-century infancy. As we have come to understand the genetics of flower colour, the odds of obtaining the colours we desire in flowers have increased.

Flower-head mutants are frequently the product of changes in floral symmetry. Typical sunflower heads have bilaterally symmetrical

Single and double forms of feverfew grew in 17th-century European gardens.

ray florets surrounding radially symmetrical disc florets. In sunflowers, flower symmetry is produced by a particular gene.[32] If this gene is mis-expressed, a 'flore pleno'-type head is formed, where radially symmetrical disc florets become asymmetrical. If the function of the gene is lost completely, the bilaterally symmetrical florets become radially symmetrical, producing a fistulose-type head. Changes in floral symmetry are of great scientific and economic interest, since floral symmetry has an enormous impact on the ecology of pollination.[33] In the Asteraceae, ray florets tend to increase pollinator visits and hence the production of outcrossed seed.[34]

Other frequent flower-head mutants are so-called rayless, or eradiate, forms, such as in sea aster and oxeye daisy, where the ray florets appear to have been lost. In some species, rayless heads develop ray florets. One of the most famous examples of this is radiate groundsel (see Chapter Two).

Beyond the Garden Wall

Over millennia we have transformed our environment, creating places where we want to live and then decorating them with plants. The changes we have wrought are enormous, and the price is frequently paid by the organisms with which we share the planet. Humans have extended some plant ranges far beyond that which could be achieved by natural dispersal; such plants sometimes have the opportunity to 'bite' us.

Asteraceae are botanical camp followers, opportunists capable of colonizing the habitats we have created and hitching lifts as we or our animals move. Under our pampering hand, horticultural Asteraceae have been deliberately moved away from their cradles of origin. In other cases, movement has been accidental. Some plants have escaped our control and threaten our food supplies, economies or environments; they have become weeds, and, perhaps more menacingly, invasives. Most Asteraceae outside their native ranges do not take hold on alien shores. Some of the immigrants – the adventives – grow but die out within a few generations. Others are more persistent, becoming naturalized and taking on the appearance of native species. Finally, a few naturalized species become prominent in their new homes; these vigorous and prolific invasives can cause enormous environmental and economic damage. However, just by looking at a species it is impossible to tell what its fate will be if it is introduced. The best one can do is to look at probabilities; approximately one in every hundred plant introductions will become invasive.[35]

There are about 2,500 naturalized species in the British Isles, nearly half of which have been introduced via horticulture.[36] Over the past three centuries the largely unregulated movement of plants into Britain for horticulture has affected the islands' flora dramatically. For example, the most widespread naturalized species in the British Isles is pineapple weed, a plant with inconspicuous flower heads and finely divided, aromatic leaves. It was first recorded in 1869 near Kew, where it appears to have arrived from North America via its native East Asia. Despite lacking an obvious mechanism for dispersal, the seeds are readily carried around in mud caked on feet and vehicles. In general, before the First World War, the number of naturalized species in Britain increased exponentially, but after the war it declined, a decline associated with the reduction in the number of large gardens and people working in them.[37]

As we have seen, Oxford ragwort, which was introduced to the Oxford Physic Garden in the early eighteenth century, eventually escaped on to the city's walls.[38] By the start of the nineteenth century Oxford ragwort was 'very plentiful on almost every wall in and around Oxford', although populations fluctuated, since 'in 1875, we only knew of it growing on walls in the corner of the town known as Jericho.'[39] The ragwort adapted slowly to its English home, although its adaptation to Scottish life took less than fifty years.[40] Subsequent events showed that Oxford ragwort was confined to the city since there was no ready means of escape and no suitable habitat outside.

The arrival of the railway in 1840s Oxford dramatically changed the ability of ragwort to escape, and track ballast proved to be an ideal home for it. Before the Second World War, most of the expansion of Oxford ragwort's British range happened to the south and west of a line connecting Liverpool and Oxford, and after 1945 major expansion occurred to the east and north of the line. The species' north-western spread has been associated with the Great Western Railway, and romanticized descriptions of plumed ragwort seeds being transported in steam-train carriages have fuelled that idea.[41] After the Second World War bomb sites provided additional habitat for the expansion of Oxford ragwort, particularly in the south and east of England.[42] The development of the road network in the 1960s probably contributed to the spread of the species, as it did for other European ragworts.[43] The expansion of Oxford ragwort has occasionally been accompanied by concerns over its extinction. In the mid-nineteenth century the plant became extinct in Worcester owing to redevelopment, while the 'ravages of collectors' and destruction during 'tidying up and setting to rights' was a problem for the population on the walls of Canterbury Cathedral in the late nineteenth century.[44]

The idea of globalization has become a cliché, but the opportunities for Asteraceae to travel across continents to exploit the habitats

The creeping South American carpet burweed, which has become a serious weed in parts of North America, Australia and Europe.

we have created are now immense. Deliberate movement of Asteraceae into gardens is unlikely to be a major worry until they escape. Unfortunately, we do not know if and when they will get into the wild, or what will happen when they are there. Once species have become invasive they can be very difficult to control, since they evolve to fit in with our lifestyles.

We have seen how one of the largest and most diverse families of flowering plants on the planet has become part of human cultures. However, only ten species in the whole sunflower family are significant sources of food for us and our animals.[45] Contrast this with the similarly sized pea family, of which there are about twenty globally important food plants. The question naturally arises: why are so few Asteraceae used for food?[46] Does the family's biology limit its ability to be domesticated? Did the decisions made by early farmers, influenced by species biology and informed by conservative food habits, channel our domestication of Asteraceae?

The chemical diversity of the Asteraceae makes them valuable as drugs but perhaps limits their food value. Reducing toxic chemicals (often associated with bitterness) through unconscious selection is a risky business, especially when food rewards are low. Selection has produced lettuce cultivars with low bitterness, but in chicory and endive bitterness has remained a desired trait. The risk of death cannot be the only reason few Asteraceae are used as foods, since major food plants have been domesticated in highly toxic families, for example potatoes and tomatoes in the Solanaceae and cassava in the Euphorbiaceae. Similarly, arguments based on the avoidance of allergens have limited credence, since highly allergenic grasses are among the world's most important food plants.

The limited energy value of Asteraceae may be the most significant reason they are generally unimportant as food. Asteraceae seed oils produce unsaturated fatty acid-rich oils that do not store well; early farmers may have preferred energy-rich species that kept better. The primary Asteraceae storage carbohydrates are indigestible fructans rather than digestible starch. Slow cooking of fructan-rich tubers may increase their calorific value, but overall food value is low compared to the effort required to evolve food-processing technology. Ultimately, the apparent lack of interest in Asteraceae as food may simply stem from the fact that we are very conservative in our food choices.

Appendix: Plant Names

Scientific names for all common names used in the text are presented here. For non-asteraceous plants and animals, family names are given. In the case of the Asteraceae, subfamilies are indicated.

alecost	*Tanacetum balsamita* (subfamily Asteroideae)
anil de Pernambuco	*Koanophyllon tinctoria* (subfamily Asteroideae)
arnica	*Arnica montana* (subfamily Asteroideae)
artemisia, annual	*Artemisia annua* (subfamily Asteroideae)
artichoke, globe	*Cynara cardunculus* var. *scolymus* (subfamily Carduoideae)
artichoke, Jerusalem	*Helianthus tuberosus* (subfamily Asteroideae)
aster	*Aster* spp. *sensu lato* (subfamily Asteroideae)
aster, China	*Callistephus chinensis* (subfamily Asteroideae)
aster, sea	*Aster tripolium* (subfamily Asteroideae)
baccharis	*Baccharis* spp. (subfamily Asteroideae)
bee-fly	*Megapalpus nitidus* (order Diptera, family Bombyliidae)
beggartick	*Bidens* spp. (subfamily Asteroideae)
beggartick, cosmos-flowered	*Bidens cosmoides* (subfamily Asteroideae)
belladonna	*Atropa belladonna* (Solanaceae)
bellflower	*Campanula* spp. (Campanulaceae)
bitou bush	*Chrysanthemoides monilifera* (subfamily Asteroideae)
bitter-leaf	*Vernonia amygdalina* (subfamily Cichorioideae)
blazing star	*Liatris* spp. (subfamily Asteroideae)
blazing star, scaly	*Liatris squarrosa* (subfamily Asteroideae)
bogbean	*Menyanthes* spp. (Menyanthaceae)
boneset	*Eupatorium* spp. (subfamily Asteroideae)
bristly oxtongue	*Helminthotheca echioides* (subfamily Asteroideae)
burdock	*Arctium* spp. (subfamily Carduoideae)
bur-marigolds	*Bidens* spp. (subfamily Asteroideae)
butterbur	*Petasites hybridus* (subfamily Carduoideae)

cabbage	*Brassica* spp. (Brassicaceae)
camomile	*Chamaemelum nobile* (subfamily Asteroideae)
camomile, German	*Matricaria recutita* (subfamily Asteroideae)
camomile, yellow	*Cota tinctoria* (subfamily Asteroideae)
camphor bush	*Tarchonanthus camphoratus* (subfamily Mutisioideae)
camphorweed	*Heterotheca subaxillaris* ssp. *latifolia* (subfamily Asteroideae)
cankerweed	*Jacobaea vulgaris* (subfamily Asteroideae)
cardoon, cultivated	*Cynara cardunculus* var. *altilis* (subfamily Carduoideae)
cardoon, wild	*Cynara cardunculus* var. *sylvestris* (subfamily Carduoideae)
carnation	*Dianthus* spp. (Caryophyllaceae)
carpet burweed	*Soliva stolonifera* (subfamily Asteroideae)
cassava	*Manihot esculenta* (Euphorbiaceae)
cat's ear	*Hypochaeris radicata* (subfamily Cichorioideae)
cat's ear, smooth	*Hypochaeris glabra* (subfamily Cichorioideae)
chicory	*Cichorium intybus* (subfamily Cichorioideae)
chrysanthemum	*Chrysanthemum* spp. (subfamily Asteroideae)
chrysanthemum, Dalmatian	*Tanacetum cinerariifolium* (subfamily Asteroideae)
cinnabar moth	*Tyria jacobaeae* (order Lepidoptera, family Arctiinae)
cocklebur	*Xanthium* spp. (subfamily Asteroideae)
coffee	*Coffea arabica* (Rubiaceae)
coltsfoot	*Tussilago farfara* (subfamily Asteroideae)
compass plant	*Silphium laciniatum* (subfamily Asteroideae)
coneflower	*Rudbeckia* spp. (subfamily Asteroideae)
coneflower, pale purple	*Echinacea pallida* (subfamily Asteroideae)
cornflower	*Centaurea cyanus* (subfamily Carduoideae)
costmary	*Tanacetum balsamita* (subfamily Asteroideae)
cotton thistle	*Onopordum acanthium* (subfamily Carduoideae)
cucumber	*Cucumis* spp. (Cucurbitaceae)
cucumber, prickly	*Echinocystis lobata* (Cucurbitaceae)
cudweed	*Gnaphalium* spp. (subfamily Asteroideae)
dahlia	*Dahlia* spp. (subfamily Asteroideae)
daisy, African	*Gerbera* spp. (subfamily Mutisioideae)
daisy, beetle	*Gorteria diffusa* (subfamily Cichorioideae)
daisy, common	*Bellis perennis* (subfamily Asteroideae)
daisy, kingfisher	*Felicia bergeriana* (subfamily Asteroideae)
daisy, Michaelmas	*Aster* spp. (subfamily Asteroideae)
daisy, oxeye	*Leucanthemum vulgare* (subfamily Asteroideae)
daisy, rain	*Dimorphotheca pluvialis* (subfamily Asteroideae)
daisy, Transvaal	*Gerbera jamesonii* (subfamily Mutisioideae)
daisy bush, New Zealand	*Olearia* spp. (subfamily Asteroideae)
dandelion	*Taraxacum* spp. (subfamily Cichorioideae)

dandelion, Russian	*Taraxacum kok-saghyz* (subfamily Cichorioideae)
dock	*Rumex* spp. (Polygonaceae)
dock, prairie	*Silphium terebinthinaceum* (subfamily Asteroideae)
echinacea	*Echinacea purpurea* (subfamily Asteroideae)
edelweiss	*Leontopodium nivale* ssp. *alpinum* (subfamily Asteroideae)
endive	*Cichorium* spp. (subfamily Cichorioideae)
everlasting	*Helichrysum* spp. (subfamily Asteroideae)
everlasting, Cape	*Syncarpha vestita* (subfamily Asteroideae)
fairies' horse	*Jacobaea vulgaris* (subfamily Asteroideae)
false aster, decurrent	*Boltonia decurrens* (subfamily Asteroideae)
felicia	*Felicia* spp. (subfamily Asteroideae)
feverfew	*Tanacetum parthenium* (subfamily Asteroideae)
fly flower	*Jacobaea vulgaris* (subfamily Asteroideae)
frailejón	subtribe Espeletiinae (subfamily Asteroideae)
gallant soldier	*Galinsoga parviflora* (subfamily Asteroideae)
gentian	*Gentiana* spp. (Gentianaceae)
gerbera	*Gerbera* spp. (subfamily Mutisioideae)
goodenia	*Goodenia* spp. (Goodeniaceae)
groundsel	*Senecio vulgaris* (subfamily Asteroideae)
groundsel, giant	*Dendrosenecio* spp. (subfamily Asteroideae)
groundsel, radiate	*Senecio vulgaris* ssp. *vulgaris* var. *hibernicus* (subfamily Asteroideae)
groundsel, sticky	*Senecio viscosus* (subfamily Asteroideae)
groundsel, York	*Senecio eboracensis* (subfamily Asteroideae)
guaco	*Mikania glomerata* (subfamily Asteroideae)
guayule	*Parthenium argentatum* (subfamily Asteroideae)
hawkbit	*Leontodon* spp. (subfamily Cichorioideae)
hawkbit, autumn	*Scorzoneroides autumnalis* (subfamily Cichorioideae)
hawksbeard, rough	*Crepis biennis* (subfamily Cichorioideae)
hawkweed	*Hieracium* spp. (subfamily Cichorioideae)
hawkweed, narrow-leaved	*Hieracium umbellatum* (subfamily Cichorioideae)
hawkweed, wall	*Hieracium murorum* (subfamily Cichorioideae)
he-cabbage tree	*Pladaroxylon leucadendron* (subfamily Asteroideae)
hop	*Humulus lupulus* (Cannabaceae)
island-aster	*Hesperomannia* spp. (subfamily Asteroideae)
Jack-go-to-bed-at-noon	*Tragopogon pratensis* (subfamily Cichorioideae)
Kew weed	*Galinsoga parviflora* (subfamily Asteroideae)
kleinia	*Kleinia* spp. (subfamily Asteroideae)
knapweed	*Centaurea* spp. (subfamily Carduoideae)
lady's mantle	*Alchemilla* spp. (Rosaceae)
lavender cotton	*Santolina chamaecyparissus* (subfamily Asteroideae)
leopard's bane, great	*Doronicum pardalianches* (subfamily Asteroideae)
lettuce, bitter	*Lactuca virosa* (subfamily Cichorioideae)
lettuce, cultivated	*Lactuca sativa* (subfamily Cichorioideae)

lettuce, wild	*Lactuca virosa* (subfamily Cichorioideae)
ligularia	*Ligularia* spp. (subfamily Asteroideae)
madder	*Rubia tinctoria* (Rubiaceae)
marefart	*Jacobaea vulgaris* (subfamily Asteroideae)
marguerite	*Argyranthemum frutescens* (subfamily Asteroideae)
marigold	*Calendula* spp. (subfamily Asteroideae)
marigold, African	*Tagetes erecta* (subfamily Asteroideae)
marigold, Cape	*Dimorphotheca sinuata* (subfamily Asteroideae)
marigold, common	*Calendula officinalis* (subfamily Asteroideae)
marigold, corn	*Glebionis segetum* (subfamily Asteroideae)
marigold, French	*Tagetes patula* (subfamily Asteroideae)
marsh elder	*Iva* spp. (subfamily Asteroideae)
marsh elder, annual	*Iva annua* (subfamily Asteroideae)
milk thistle, blessed	*Silybum marianum* (subfamily Carduoideae)
milk thistle, purple	*Galactites tomentosa* (subfamily Carduoideae)
mint, black	*Tagetes minuta* (subfamily Asteroideae)
muggart	*Jacobaea vulgaris* (subfamily Asteroideae)
mugwort	*Artemisia vulgaris* (subfamily Asteroideae)
niger	*Guizotia abyssinica* (subfamily Asteroideae)
oak	*Quercus* spp. (Fagaceae)
oak leaf plant, Mexican	*Shinnersia rivularis* (subfamily Asteroideae)
oil palm	*Elaeis guineensis* (Arecaceae)
othonna	*Othonna* spp. (subfamily Asteroideae)
periwinkle, rosy	*Catharanthus roseus* (Apocynaceae)
pineapple weed	*Matricaria discoidea* (subfamily Asteroideae)
piss-a-bed	*Taraxacum* spp. (subfamily Cichorioideae)
pissenlit	*Taraxacum* spp. (subfamily Cichorioideae)
poppy	*Papaver rhoeas* (Papaveraceae)
potato	*Solanum tuberosum* (Solanaceae)
potato, Canadian	*Helianthus tuberosus* (subfamily Asteroideae)
quinine	*Cinchona* spp. (Rubiaceae)
ragweed	*Ambrosia* spp. (subfamily Asteroideae)
ragweed, Barbary	*Hertia cheirifolia* (subfamily Asteroideae)
ragwort, common	*Jacobaea vulgaris* (subfamily Asteroideae)
ragwort, Oxford	*Senecio squalidus* (subfamily Asteroideae)
ragwort, Welsh	*Senecio cambrensis* (subfamily Asteroideae)
rape	*Brassica napus* (Brassicaceae)
rice	*Oryza sativa* (Poaceae)
rose	*Rosa* spp. (Rosaceae)
rubber tree	*Hevea brasiliensis* (Euphorbiaceae)
safflower	*Carthamus tinctorius* (subfamily Carduoideae)
saffron	*Crocus sativus* (Iridaceae)
saffron, bastard	*Carthamus tinctorius* (subfamily Carduoideae)
saffron, dyer's	*Carthamus tinctorius* (subfamily Carduoideae)
St Paul's wort	*Sigesbeckia orientalis* (subfamily Asteroideae)
saw-wort	*Saussurea* spp. (subfamily Carduoideae)

saw-wort	*Serratula tinctoria* (subfamily Carduoideae)
senecio	*Senecio* spp. *sensu lato* (subfamily Asteroideae)
she-cabbage tree	*Lachanodes arborea* (subfamily Asteroideae)
shit-a-bed	*Taraxacum* spp. (subfamily Cichorioideae)
shungiku	*Chrysanthemum coronarium* (subfamily Asteroideae)
silversword	*Argyroxiphium* spp. (subfamily Asteroideae)
snakeplant	*Nassauvia serpens* (subfamily Mutisioideae)
snow lotus	*Saussurea laniceps* (subfamily Carduoideae)
sowthistle	*Sonchus* spp. (subfamily Cichorioideae)
sowthistle, common	*Sonchus oleraceus* (subfamily Cichorioideae)
sowthistle, prickly	*Sonchus asper* (subfamily Cichorioideae)
soya	*Glycine max* (Fabaceae)
staggerwort	*Jacobaea vulgaris* (subfamily Asteroideae)
stevia	*Stevia rebaudiana* (subfamily Asteroideae)
strawberry	*Fragaria* spp. (Rosaceae)
succory, yellow	*Catananche lutea* (subfamily Cichorioideae)
sunflower	*Helianthus* spp. (subfamily Asteroideae)
sunflower, common	*Helianthus annuus* (subfamily Asteroideae)
sunflower, desert	*Helianthus deserticola* (subfamily Asteroideae)
sunflower, false	*Phoebanthus* spp. (subfamily Asteroideae)
sunflower, paradox	*Helianthus paradoxus* (subfamily Asteroideae)
sunflower, prairie	*Helianthus petiolaris* (subfamily Asteroideae)
sunflower, western	*Helianthus anomalus* (subfamily Asteroideae)
tansy	*Tanacetum vulgare* (subfamily Asteroideae)
tarragon, French	*Artemisia dracunculus* (subfamily Asteroideae)
tarragon, Russian	*Artemisia dracunculoides* (subfamily Asteroideae)
thale cress	*Arabidopsis thaliana* (Brassicaceae)
thistle	subfamily Carduoideae
thistle, blessed	*Centaurea benedicta* (subfamily Carduoideae)
thistle, carline	*Carlina vulgaris* (subfamily Carduoideae)
thistle, globe	*Echinops* spp. (subfamily Carduoideae)
thistle, holy	*Centaurea benedicta* (subfamily Carduoideae)
thistle, woolly	*Cirsium eriophorum* (subfamily Carduoideae)
tickseed, golden	*Coreopsis tinctoria* (subfamily Asteroideae)
toothache plant	*Acmella oleracea* (subfamily Asteroideae)
tubú	*Montanoa guatemalensis* (subfamily Asteroideae)
verode	*Kleinia neriifolia* (subfamily Asteroideae)
weld	*Reseda luteola* (Resedaceae)
wingpetal	*Heterosperma pinnatum* (subfamily Asteroideae)
woad	*Isatis tinctoria* (Brassicaceae)
wormwood	*Artemisia* spp. (subfamily Asteroideae)
wormwood, common	*Artemisia absinthium* (subfamily Asteroideae)
yacón	*Smallanthus sonchifolius* (subfamily Asteroideae)
yarrow	*Achillea* spp. (subfamily Asteroideae)
yarrow	*Achillea millefolium* (subfamily Asteroideae)
yew, Pacific	*Taxus brevifolia* (Taxaceae)

References

1 Amazing

1 Quoted in C. B. Heiser et al., 'The North American Sunflowers (*Helianthus*)', *Memoirs of the Torrey Botanical Club*, XXII (1969), pp. 1–218.

2 J. Gerarde, *The Herball or Generall Historie of Plantes* (London, 1597), pp. 612–14.

3 BBC News, On this Day, 11 November 1987, http://news.bbc.co.uk (accessed 1 May 2016).

4 Dutch Safety Board, Investigation Crash MH17, 17 July 2014, Donetsk, www.onderzoeksraad.nl (accessed 1 April 2016).

5 S. Knapton, 'Micro-gravity Gardening: First Flower Blooms in Space', *The Telegraph*, 18 January 2016, www.telegraph.co.uk.

6 Gerarde, *The Herball*, p. 612.

7 Many excellent time-lapse clips of germinating sunflower seeds and of opening sunflower inflorescences (and other Asteraceae) are available online.

8 Wilhelm Pfeffer, *Studies of Plant Movement, 1898–1900*, Kinetoscope Archives, www.dailymotion.com (accessed 1 April 2016).

9 C. Darwin, *The Power of Movement in Plants* (London, 1880).

10 D. Israelsson and A. Johnsson, 'A Theory for Circumnutations in *Helianthus annuus*', *Physiologia Plantarum*, XX (1967), pp. 957–76.

11 Common names will be used where possible; a complete list of scientific equivalents is given in the Appendix.

12 A. Johnsson et al., 'Gravity Amplifies and Microgravity Decreases Circumnutations in *Arabidopsis thaliana* Stems: Results from a Space Experiment', *New Phytologist*, CLXXXII (2009), pp. 621–9.

13 Gerarde, *The Herball*, p. 613.

14 P. D. Hurd et al., 'Principal Sunflower Bees of North America with Emphasis on the Southwestern United States (Hymenoptera: Apoidea)', *Smithsonian Contributions to Zoology*, CCCX (1980), pp. 1–158; R. L. Minckley et al., 'Behavior and Phenology of a Specialist Bee (*Dieunomia*) and Sunflower (*Helianthus*) Pollen Availability', *Ecology*, LXXV (1994), pp. 1406–19.

15 L. H. Rieseberg, 'Hybrid Speciation in Wild Sunflowers', *Annals of the Missouri Botanical Garden*, XCIII (2006), pp. 34–48.

16 H. M. Alexander and A. M. Schrag, 'Role of Soil Seed Banks and Newly Dispersed Seeds in Population Dynamics of the Annual Sunflower, *Helianthus annuus*', *Journal of Ecology*, XCI (2003), pp. 987–98.

2 Varying

1   W. H. Baxter, 'Vegetation of the Paramos of New Grenada', *The Garden*, XI (1877), p. 408.

2   W. Baxter, 'Botanical Excursions in 1812', unpublished manuscript (Druce Archive 37.1, Sherardian Library of Plant Taxonomy, Oxford).

3   J.E.M. Watson et al., 'Catastrophic Declines in Wilderness Areas Undermine Global Environment Targets', *Current Biology*, XXVI (2016), pp. 1–6.

4   J. Ruel, *De Natura Stirpium Libri Tres* (Basle, 1536); G. Hardy and L. Totelin, *Ancient Botany* (London, 2016).

5   J. M. Bonifacino et al., 'A History of Research in Compositae: Early Beginnings to the Reading Meeting (1975)', in V. A. Funk et al., *Systematics, Evolution, and Biogeography of Compositae* (Vienna, 2009), pp. 3–38.

6   B. Thiers, *Index Herbariorum: A Global Directory of Public Herbaria and Associated Staff. New York Botanical Garden's Virtual Herbarium*, http://sweetgum.nybg.org (accessed 10 May 2016).

7   Z. A. Goodwin et al., 'Widespread Mistaken Identity in Tropical Plant Collections', *Current Biology*, XXV (2015), pp. 1066–7; D. P. Bebber et al., 'Herbaria Are a Major Frontier for Species Discovery', *Proceedings of the National Academy of Sciences USA*, CVII (2010), pp. 22169–71.

8   Goodwin, 'Widespread Mistaken Identity'.

9   C. E. Raven, *John Ray: Naturalist, His Life and Works* (Cambridge, 1950).

10 P. H. Oswald and C. D. Preston, *John Ray's Cambridge Catalogue (1660)* (London, 2011).

11 Bonifacino, 'A History of Research in Compositae', p. 5.

12 B. B. Fontenelle, 'Eloge de M. de Tournefort', *Histoire de l'Académie Royale des Sciences*, MMMCDLXXXIV (1708), pp. 143–54 (author's translation).

13 H. W. Lack with D. J. Mabberley, *The Flora Graeca Story: Sibthorp, Bauer, and Hawkins in the Levant* (Oxford, 1999).

14 G. Gardner, *Travels in the Interior of Brazil, Principally Through the Northern Provinces, and the Gold and Diamond Districts, During the Years 1836–1841* (London, 1849).

15 D.J.N. Hind, 'Determinations of George Gardner's Compositae from Brazil' (London, 2012), available at www.kew.org.

16 W. Dean, *Brazil and the Struggle for Rubber: A Study in Environmental History* (Cambridge, 1987).

17 D. F. Robinson, *Confronting Biopiracy: Challenges, Cases and International Debates* (London, 2012).

18 B. W. Ogilvie, *The Science of Describing: Natural History in Renaissance Europe* (Chicago, IL, 2006).

19 S. A. Harris, 'Introduction of Oxford Ragwort, *Senecio squalidus*
    L.(Asteraceae), to the United Kingdom', *Watsonia*, XXIV (2002),
    pp. 31–43.

20 K. Thomas, *Man and the Natural World: Changing Attitudes in England, 1500–1800*
    (London, 1983).

21 U. Eliasson, 'Studies in Galapagos Plants. XIV. The Genus *Scalesia* Arn.',
    Opera Botanica, XXXVI (1974), pp. 1–117.

22 H. J. Noltie, 'The Generic Name *Scalesia* (Compositae) – An
    Etymological Blunder', *Archives of Natural History*, XXXIX (2012), pp. 167–9.

23 K. Bremer, *Asteraceae: Cladistics and Classification* (Portland, OR, 1994).

24 D. S. Soltis et al., *Phylogeny and Evolution of Angiosperms* (Sunderland, MA,
    2005), pp. 224–5.

25 A. G. Morton, *History of Botanical Science: An Account of the Development of Botany
    from Ancient Times to the Present Day* (London, 1981); V. Žárský and J. Tupý,
    'A Missed Anniversary: 300 Years after Rudolf Jacob Camerarius' "De
    Sexu Plantarum Epistola"', *Sexual Plant Reproduction*, VIII (1995), pp. 375–6.

26 Bonifacino, 'A History of Research in Compositae', pp. 3–38.

27 R. M. King and H. Dawson, *Cassini on Compositae* (New York, 1975).

28 T. E. Wood, 'The Frequency of Polyploid Speciation in Vascular Plants',
    Proceedings of the National Academy of Sciences USA, CVI (2009), pp. 13875–9.

29 Funk, *Systematics*.

30 R. K. Jansen and J. D. Palmer, 'A Chloroplast DNA Inversion Marks
    an Ancient Evolutionary Split in the Sunflower Family (Asteraceae)',
    Proceedings of the National Academy of Sciences USA, LXXXIV (1987), pp. 5818–22.

31 V. D. Barreda et al., 'Eocene Patagonia Fossils of the Daisy Family', *Science*,
    CCCXXIX (2010), p. 1621.

32 V. D. Barreda et al., 'Early Evolution of the Angiosperm Clade Asteraceae
    in the Cretaceous of Antarctica', *Proceedings of the National Academy of Sciences
    USA*, CXII (2015), pp. 10989–94.

33 B. G. Baldwin, 'Heliantheae Alliance', in Funk, *Systematics*, pp. 689–711.

34 E. E. Schilling et al., 'Phylogenetic Relationships in *Helianthus* (Asteraceae)
    Based on Nuclear Ribosomal DNA Internal Transcribed Spacer Region
    Sequence Data', *Systematic Botany*, XXIII (1998), pp. 177–87.

35 C. B. Heiser et al., 'The North American Sunflowers (*Helianthus*)', *Memoirs
    of the Torrey Botanical Club*, XXII (1969), pp. 1–218.

36 C. A. Stace et al., *Hybrid Flora of the British Isles* (Bristol, 2015).

37 R. J. Abbott and A. J. Lowe, 'Origins, Establishment and Evolution of
    New Polyploid Species: *Senecio cambrensis* and *S. eboracensis* in the British
    Isles', *Biological Journal of the Linnean Society*, LXXXII (2004), pp. 467–74;
    R. J. Abbott and D. G. Forbes, 'Extinction of the Edinburgh Lineage
    of the Allopolyploid Neospecies, *Senecio cambrensis* Rosser (Asteraceae)',
    Heredity, LXXXVIII (2002), pp. 267–9.

38 A. J. Lowe and R. J. Abbott, 'Routes of Origin of Two Recently Evolved
    Hybrid Taxa: *Senecio vulgaris* var. *hibernicus* and York Radiate Groundsel
    (Asteraceae)', *American Journal of Botany*, LXXXVII (2000), pp. 1159–67.

39 Ibid.

40 J. E. Lousley, 'A New Hybrid *Senecio* from the London Area', *Botanical Exchange Club Report*, XII (1946), pp. 869–74.

41 L. H. Rieseberg, 'Hybrid Speciation in Wild Sunflowers', *Annals of the Missouri Botanical Garden*, XCIII (2006), pp. 34–48.

42 J. K. James and R. J. Abbott, 'Recent, Allopatric, Homoploid Hybrid Speciation: The Origin of *Senecio Squalidus* (Asteraceae) in the British Isles from a Hybrid Zone on Mount Etna, Sicily', *Evolution*, LIX (2005), pp. 2533–47.

3 Surviving

1 E.A.N. Arber, *Plant Life in Alpine Switzerland: Being an Account in Simple Language of the Natural History of Alpine Plants* (London, 1910), pp. 15–17.

2 S. Carlquist, *Island Biology* (New York, 1974).

3 Q.C.B. Cronk, *The Endemic Flora of St Helena* (Oswestry, 1995).

4 S. C. Kim et al., 'A Common Origin for Woody *Sonchus* and Five Related Genera in the Macaronesian Islands: Molecular Evidence for Extensive Radiation', *Proceedings of the National Academy of Sciences USA*, XCIII (1996), pp. 7743–8.

5 F. Lens et al., 'Insular Woodiness on the Canary Islands: A Remarkable Case Study of Parallel Evolution', *International Journal of Plant Sciences*, CLXXIV (2013), pp. 992–1013.

6 A. von Humboldt and A. Bonpland, *Essay on the Geography of Plants* (Chicago, IL, 2009).

7 R. Spruce, *Notes of a Botanist on the Amazon and Andes, Being Records of Travel on the Amazon and Its Tributaries . . . During the Years 1849–1864* (London, 1908), p. 288.

8 J. Small, 'The Origin and Development of the Compositae', *New Phytologist*, XVIII (1919), p. 142.

9 J. Nakajima et al., 'Asteraceae: Lista de Espécies da Flora do Brasil', www.floradobrasil.jbrj.gov.br (accessed 11 June 2016).

10 A. Shmida, 'Biogeography of the Desert Flora', in *Ecosystems of the World*, ed. M. Evenari et al., vol. XIIA (Amsterdam, 1985), pp. 23–77.

11 W. J. Burchell, *Travels in the Interior of Southern Africa*, vol. I (London, 1822), p. 284.

12 C. Raunkiær, *The Life Forms of Plants and Statistical Plant Geography, Being the Collected Papers of C. Raunkiær* (Oxford, 1934).

13 A. Erhardt, 'Pollination of the Edelweiss, *Leontopodium alpinum*', *Botanical Journal of the Linnean Society*, CXI (1993), pp. 229–40.

14 B. G. Gardiner, 'Linnaeus's Floral Clock', *The Linnean*, III (1987), pp. 26–9.

15 C. Linnaeus, *Philisophia Botanica* (Stockholm, 1751), pp. 274–5.

16 M. Proctor et al., *The Natural History of Pollination* (London, 1996).

17 A. G. Ellis and S. D. Johnson, 'Floral Mimicry Enhances Pollen Export: The Evolution of Pollination by Sexual Deceit Outside of the Orchidaceae', *American Naturalist*, CLXXVI (2010), pp. 143–51; S. Johnson and J. Midgley, 'Fly Pollination of *Gorteria diffusa* (Asteraceae), and a

Possible Mimetic Function for Dark Spots on the Capitulum', *American Journal of Botany*, LXXXIV (1997), pp. 429–36.

18   S. Vogel, 'Vertebrate Pollination in Compositae: Floral Syndromes and Field Observations', *Stapfia*, CIII (2015), pp. 5–26.

19   P. E. Berry and R. N. Calvo, 'Wind Pollination, Self-incompatibility, and Altitudinal Shifts in Pollination Systems in the High Andean Genus *Espeletia* (Asteraceae)', *American Journal of Botany*, LXXVI (1989), pp. 1602–14.

20   P. J. van Dijk et al., 'An Apomixis-gene's View on Dandelions', in *Lost Sex: The Evolutionary Biology of Parthenogenesis*, ed. I. Schön et al. (Berlin, 2009), pp. 475–95.

21   J. C. Sheldon and F. M. Burrows, 'The Dispersal Effectiveness of the Achene-pappus Units of Selected Compositae in Steady Winds with Convection', *New Phytologist*, LXXII (1973), pp. 665–75; V. Casseau et al., 'Morphologic and Aerodynamic Considerations Regarding the Plumed Seeds of *Tragopogon pratensis* and Their Implications for Seed Dispersal', *PLOS One*, X (2015), p. e0125040.

22   K. Faegri and L. van der Pijl, *The Principles of Pollination Ecology* (Oxford, 1979).

23   M. Smith and T. M. Keevin, 'Achene Morphology, Production and Germination, and Potential for Water Dispersal in *Boltonia decurrens* (Decurrent False Aster), a Threatened Floodplain Species', *Rhodora*, CDI (1998), pp. 69–81.

24   C. A. Backer, *The Problem of Krakatoa as Seen by a Botanist* (Sourabaya, Java, 1929).

25   F. R. Ganders et al., 'Its Base Sequence Phylogeny in *Bidens* (Asteraceae): Evidence for the Continental Relatives of Hawaiian and Marquesan *Bidens*', *Systematic Botany*, XXV (2000), pp. 122–33; M. L. Knope et al., 'Area and the Rapid Radiation of Hawaiian *Bidens* (Asteraceae)', *Journal of Biogeography*, XXXIX (2012), pp. 1206–16; S. Carlquist, 'The Biota of Long-distance Dispersal. III: Loss of Dispersibility in the Hawaiian Flora', *Brittonia*, XVIII (1966), pp. 310–35.

26   M. L. Cody and J. M. Overton, 'Short-term Evolution of Reduced Dispersal in Island Plant Populations', *Journal of Ecology*, LXXXIV (1996), pp. 53–61.

27   C. Martorell and M. Martínez-López, 'Informed Dispersal in Plants: *Heterosperma pinnatum* (Asteraceae) Adjusts Its Dispersal Mode to Escape from Competition and Water Stress', *Oikos*, CXXIII (2014), pp. 225–31.

28   D. L. Venable and D. A. Levin, 'Ecology of Achene Dimorphism in *Heterotheca latifolia*. I: Achene Structure, Germination and Dispersal', *Journal of Ecology*, LXXIII (1985), pp. 133–45.

29   E. Imbert and O. Ronce, 'Phenotypic Plasticity for Dispersal Ability in the Seed Heteromorphic *Crepis sancta* (Asteraceae)', *Oikos*, XCIII (2001), pp. 126–34; P. B. McEvoy and C. S. Cox, 'Wind Dispersal Distances in Dimorphic Achenes of Ragwort, *Senecio jacobaea*', *Ecology*, LXVIII (1987), pp. 2006–15.

30 E. Ruiz de Clavijo and M. J. Jiménez, 'The Influence of Achene Type and Plant Density on Growth and Biomass Allocation in the Heterocarpic Annual *Catanache lutea* (Asteraceae)', *International Journal of Plant Sciences*, CLIX (1998), pp. 637–47.

31 O. Hedberg, 'Features of Afroalpine Plant Ecology', *Acta Phytogeographica Suecica*, XLIX (1964), pp. 1–14.

32 F. A. Squeo et al., 'Freezing Tolerance and Avoidance in High Tropical Andean Plants: Is It Equally Represented in Species with Different Plant Height?', *Oecologia*, LXXXVI (1991), pp. 378–82; U. Lüttge, *Physiological Ecology of Tropical Plants* (Berlin, 1997), pp. 321–47.

33 J. P. Vigneron et al., 'Optical Structure and Function of the White Filamentary Hair Covering the Edelweiss Bracts', *Physical Review*, E.71, (2005), p. 011906.

34 E. Beck et al., 'Estimation of Leaf and Stem Growth of Unbranched *Senecio keniodendron* Trees', *Flora*, CLXX (1980), pp. 68–76.

35 M. Acosta-Solís, *Los Páramos Andinos del Ecuador* (Quito, 1984).

36 P. J. Melcher, 'Determinants of Thermal Balance in the Hawaiian Giant Rosette Plant, *Argyroxiphium sandwicense*', *Oecologia*, XCVIII (1994), pp. 412–18.

37 Y. Yang and H. Sun, 'The Bracts of *Saussurea velutina* (Asteraceae) Protect Inflorescences from Fluctuating Weather at High Elevations of the Hengduan Mountains, Southwestern China', *Arctic, Antarctic, and Alpine Research*, XLI (2009), pp. 515–21.

38 Y. Yang et al., 'The Ecological Significance of Pubescence in *Saussurea medusa*, a High-elevation Himalayan "Woolly Plant"', *Arctic, Antarctic, and Alpine Research*, XL (2008), pp. 250–55.

39 W. Law and J. Salick, 'Human-induced Dwarfing of Himalayan Snow Lotus, *Saussurea laniceps* (Asteraceae)', *Proceedings of the National Academy of Sciences USA*, CII (2005), pp. 10218–20.

40 S. Hales, *Vegetable Staticks* (London, 1727).

41 Lüttge, *Physiological Ecology*, pp. 251–320.

42 G. Goldstein et al., 'The Role of Capacitance in the Water Balance of Andean Giant Rosette Species', *Plant, Cell and Environment*, VII (1983), pp. 179–86.

43 R. M. Cowling et al., 'Namaqualand, South Africa – An Overview of a Unique Winter-rainfall Desert Ecosystem', *Plant Ecology*, CXLII (1999), pp. 3–21.

44 M. W. van Rooyen, 'Functional Aspects of Short-lived Plants', in *The Karoo: Ecological Patterns and Processes*, ed. W.R.J. Dean and S. J. Milton (Cambridge, 1999), pp. 107–22.

45 A. D. McKown et al., 'Phylogeny of *Flaveria* (Asteraceae) and Inference of C4 Photosynthesis Evolution', *American Journal of Botany*, XCII (2005), pp. 1911–28.

46 R. F. Sage, 'The Evolution of C4 Photosynthesis', *New Phytologist*, CLXI (2004), pp. 341–70.

47 K. Winter et al., 'Crassulacean Acid Metabolism: A Continuous or Discrete Trait?', *New Phytologist*, CCVIII (2015), pp. 73–8.

48 J. Goudsblom, 'The Domestication of Fire as a Civilizing Process', *Theory, Culture, Society*, IV (1987), pp. 457–76.

49 S. J. Pyne, *Fire: Nature and Culture* (London, 2012).

50 N.A.C. Brown, 'Seed Germination in the Fynbos Fire Ephemeral, *Syncarpha vestita* (L) B. Nord. Is Promoted by Smoke, Aqueous Extracts of Smoke and Charred Wood Derived from Burning the Ericoid-leaved Shrub, *Passerina vulgaris* Thoday', *International Journal of Wildland Fire*, III (1993), pp. 203–6.

51 J. Klimešová and L. Klimeš, 'Bud Banks and Their Role in Vegetative Regeneration: A Literature Review and Proposal for Simple Classification and Assessment', *Perspectives in Plant Ecology, Evolution, and Systematics*, VIII (2007), pp. 115–29.

52 B. Appezzato-da-Glória et al., 'Underground Systems of Asteraceae Species from the Brazilian Cerrado', *Journal of the Torrey Botanical Society*, CXXXV (2008), pp. 103–13.

53 Ibid.; E. O. Joaquim et al., 'Inulin Contents and Tissue Distribution in Underground Storage Organs of Asteraceae Species from the Brazilian Rocky Fields', *Botany*, XCII (2014), pp. 827–36.

4 Curing

1 E. Trinkaus, *The Shanidar Neanderthals* (New York, 1983).

2 R. S. Solecki, 'Shanidar IV, a Neanderthal Flower Burial in Northern Iraq', *Science*, CXC (1975), pp. 880–81; A. Leroi-Gourhan, 'The Flowers Found with Shanidar IV, a Neanderthal Burial in Iraq', *Science*, CXC (1975), pp. 562–4; J. Lietava, 'Medicinal Plants in a Middle Paleolithic Grave Shanidar IV?', *Journal of Ethnopharmacology*, XXXV (1992), pp. 263–6; J. D. Sommer, 'The Shanidar IV "Flower Burial": A Re-evaluation of Neanderthal Burial Ritual', *Cambridge Archaeological Journal*, IX (1999), pp. 127–9; D. Nadel et al., 'Earliest Floral Grave Lining from 13,700–11,700-y-old Natufian Burials at Raqefet Cave, Mt. Carmel, Israel', *Proceedings of the National Academy of Sciences USA*, CX (2013), pp. 11774–8.

3 L. M. Calabria et al., 'Secondary Chemistry of Compositae', in V. A. Funk et al., *Systematics, Evolution, and Biogeography of Compositae* (Vienna, 2009), pp. 73–88.

4 B. Ebbell, *The Papyrus Ebers: The Greatest Egyptian Medical Document* (London, 1937).

5 M. A. Ibrahima et al., 'Significance of Endangered and Threatened Plant Natural Products in the Control of Human Disease', *Proceedings of the National Academy of Sciences USA*, CX (2013), pp. 16832–7.

6 J. Goodman and V. Walsh, *The Story of Taxol: Nature and Politics in the Pursuit of an Anti-cancer Drug* (Cambridge, 2006).

7 M. A. Huffman, 'Self-medicative Behavior in the African Great Apes: An Evolutionary Perspective into the Origins of Human Traditional

Medicine', *BioScience*, LI (2001), pp. 651–61; A. G. Morton, *History of Botanical Science: An Account of the Development of Botany from Ancient Times to the Present Day* (London, 1980).

8 R. W. Wrangham and T. Nishida, '*Aspilia* spp. Leaves: A Puzzle in the Feeding Behaviour of Wild Chimpanzees', *Primates*, XXIV (1983), pp. 276–82.

9 M. A. Huffman, 'Animal Self-medication and Ethno-medicine: Exploration and Exploitation of the Medicinal Properties of Plants', *Proceedings of the Nutrition Society*, LXII (2003), pp. 371–81; N. J. Toyang and R. Verpoorte, 'A Review of the Medicinal Potentials of Plants of the Genus *Vernonia* (Asteraceae)', *Journal of Ethnopharmacology*, CXLVI (2013), pp. 681–723.

10 Morton, *History of Botanical Science*.

11 M. Collins, *Medieval Herbals: The Illustrative Traditions* (London, 2000).

12 Morton, *History of Botanical Science*; D. C. Lindberg, *The Beginnings of Western Science: The European Scientific Tradition in Philosophical, Religious, and Institutional Context, Prehistory to AD 1450* (Chicago, IL, 2007), chap. 13.

13 A. Arber, *Herbals, Their Origin and Evolution: A Chapter in the History of Botany* (Cambridge, 1986).

14 T. Brasbridge, *The Poore Mans Iewell, That Is to Say, a Treatise of the Pestilence . . .* (London, 1578), pp. 36–49.

15 M. Grieve, *A Modern Herbal* (London, 1979).

16 S.-Y. Hu, *An Enumeration of Chinese Materia Medica* (Hong Kong, 1980).

17 S.W.F. Holloway, *Royal Pharmaceutical Society of Great Britain, 1841–1991: A Political and Social History* (London, 1991).

18 World Health Organization, *WHO Traditional Medicine Strategy, 2002–2005* (Geneva, 2002).

19 R. N. Bennet and R. M. Wallsgrove, 'Secondary Metabolism in Plant Defense-mechanisms', *New Phytologist*, CXXVII (1994), pp. 617–33; J. B. Harborne, 'The Comparative Biochemistry of Phytoalexin Induction in Plants', *Biochemical Systematics and Ecology*, XXVII (1999), pp. 335–67; T. Mitchell-Olds, 'Chemical Ecology in the Molecular Era', *Trends in Plant Sciences*, III (1998), pp. 362–5.

20 D. Frohne and H. J. Pfänder, *Poisonous Plants: A Handbook for Doctors, Pharmacists, Toxicologists, Biologists and Veterinarians* (London, 2004).

21 W. G. Whaley and J. S. Bowen, *Russian Dandelion (kok-saghyz): An Emergency Source of Natural Rubber* (Washington, DC, 1947).

22 D. T. Ray et al., 'Breeding Guayule for Commercial Production', *Industrial Crops and Products*, XXII (2004), pp. 15–25.

23 M. Grdiša et al., 'Genetic Diversity and Structure of Dalmatian Pyrethrum (*Tanacetum cinerariifolium* Trevir./Sch./Bip., [sic] Asteraceae) within the Balkan Refugium', *PLOS One*, IX (2014), p. e105265.

24 J. E. Arriagada, 'Ethnobotany of *Clibadium* L. (Compositae, Heliantheae) in Latin America', *Economic Botany*, XLIX (1995), pp. 328–30.

25 A.-F.M. Rizk, 'The Pyrrolizidine Alkaloids: Plant Sources and Properties', in *Naturally Occurring Pyrrolizidine Alkaloids*, ed. A.-F.M. Rizk

(Boca Raton, FL, 1991), pp. 1–89; A. R. Mattocks, *Chemistry and Toxicology of Pyrrolizidine Alkaloids* (London, 1986).

26 S. Anke et al., 'Polyphyletic Origin of Pyrrolizidine Alkaloids within the Asteraceae: Evidence from Differential Tissue Expression of Homospermidine Synthase', *Plant Physiology*, CXXXVI (2004), pp. 4037–47.

27 J. P. Dempster, 'The Population Ecology of the Cinnabar Moth, *Tyria jacobaeae* L. (Lepidoptera, Arctiidae)', *Oecologia*, VII (1982), pp. 26–67.

28 J. F. Tooker et al., 'Altered Host Plant Volatiles Are Proxies for Sex Pheromones in the Gall Wasp *Antistrophus rufus*', *Proceedings of the National Academy of Sciences USA*, XCIX (2002), pp. 15486–91.

29 V. Sharma and I. N. Sarkar, 'Leveraging Biodiversity Knowledge for Potential Phytotherapeutic Applications', *Journal of the American Medical Informatics Association*, XX (2013), pp. 668–79.

30 D. E. Allen and G. Hatfield, *Medicinal Plants in Folk Tradition: An Ethnobotany of Britain and Ireland* (Portland, OR, 2004); H. D. Neuwinger, *African Ethnobotany: Poisons and Drugs: Chemistry, Pharmacology, Toxicology* (London, 1996); D. E. Moerman, *Native American Ethnobotany* (Portland, OR, 1998); R. E. Schultes and R. F. Raffauf, *The Healing Forest: Medicinal and Toxic Plants of the Northwest Amazonia* (Portland, OR, 1990); M. Heinrich et al., 'Ethnopharmacology of Mexican Asteraceae (Compositae)', *Annual Review of Pharmacology and Toxicology*, XXXVIII (1998), pp. 539–65; P. A. Cox, 'Polynesian Herbal Medicine', in *Islands, Plants, and Polynesians: An Introduction to Polynesian Ethnobotany*, ed. P. A. Cox and A. Banack (Portland, OR, 1991), pp. 147–68.

31 R. J. Huxtable, 'The Myth of Beneficent Nature: The Risks of Herbal Preparations', *Annals of Internal Medicine*, CXVII (1992), pp. 165–6.

32 R. Turner, βοτανολογια *The British Physician: Or, the Nature and Vertues of English Plants* (London, 1687).

33 T. Bright, *A Treatise: Wherein Is Declared the Sufficiencie of English Medicines, for Cure of All Diseases, Cured with Medicine* (London, 1580). Local plants were particularly good for curing the diseases of a country's poor; see, for example, P. Dubé, *The Poor Man's Physician and Surgeon: Shewing the True Method of Curing All Sorts of Distempers . . .*, 8th edn (London, 1704).

34 B. D. Jackson, 'A Draft of a Letter by John Gerard', *Cambridge Antiquarian Communications*, IV (1881), pp. 1876–80.

35 T. Holm, 'Joan Baptista Porta', *American Naturalist*, LII (1918), pp. 455–61.

36 N. Culpeper, *The English Physician Enlarged* (London, 1656).

37 N. Culpeper, *A Physicall Directory of a Translation of the London Dispensatory* (London, 1649).

38 N. Culpeper, *The English Physician Enlarged* (London, 1666), p. 265.

39 Ibid., p. 267.

40 W. Coles, *The Art of Simpling: An Introduction to the Knowledge and Gathering of Plants* (London, 1656).

41 Y. Tu, 'The Discovery of Artemisinin (Qinghaosu) and Gifts from Chinese Medicine', *Nature Medicine*, XVII (2011), pp. 1217–20; E. Hsu, 'Qing Hao (Herba Artemisiae Annuae) in the Chinese *Materia Medica*',

in *Plants, Health and Healing: On the Interface of Ethnobotany and Medical Anthropology*, ed. E. Hsu and S. A. Harris (Oxford, 2010), pp. 83–130.

42 C. H. Saslis-Lagoudakisa et al., 'Phylogenies Reveal Predictive Power of Traditional Medicine in Bioprospecting', *Proceedings of the National Academy of Sciences USA*, CIX (2012), pp. 15835–40; F. Zhu et al., 'Clustered Patterns of Species Origins of Nature-derived Drugs and Clues for Future Bioprospecting', *Proceedings of the National Academy of Sciences USA*, CVIII (2011), pp. 12943–8.

43 PhRMA, *Biopharmaceutical Research and Development: The Process Behind New Medicines* (Washington, DC, 2015).

44 D. F. Robinson, *Confronting Biopiracy: Challenges, Cases and International Debates* (London, 2012).

45 B. Sibbald and M. Roland, 'Understanding Controlled Trials: Why Are Randomised Controlled Trials Important?', *British Medical Journal*, CCCXVI (1998), p. 201.

46 M. Heinrich et al., *Fundamentals of Pharmacognosy and Phytotherapy* (London, 2004); J. G. Evans, 'East Goes West: *Ginkgo biloba* and Dementia', in Hsu and Harris, *Plants, Health and Healing*, pp. 229–61.

47 B. Barrett, 'Medicinal Properties of *Echinacea*: A Critical Review', *Phytomedicine*, X (2003), pp. 66–86.

48 J. Le Coz and G. Ducombs, 'Plants and Plant Products', in *Contact Dermatitis*, ed. P. J. Frosch et al. (Berlin, 2006), pp. 751–800.

49 T. J. Schmidt, 'Structure-activity Relationships of Sesquiterpene Lactones', in *Studies in Natural Product Chemistry: Bioactive Natural Products (Part M)*, ed. A.-U. Rahman (Amsterdam, 2006), pp. 309–92.

50 M. Jacob et al., 'Sesquiterpene Lactone Mix as a Diagnostic Tool for Asteraceae Allergic Contact Dermatitis: Chemical Explanation for Its Poor Performance and Sesquiterpene Lactone Mix II as a Proposed Improvement', *Contact Dermatitis*, LXVI (2012), pp. 233–40.

51 N. Wopfner et al., 'The Spectrum of Allergens in Ragweed and Mugwort Pollen', *International Archives of Allergy and Immunology*, CXXXVIII (2005), pp. 337–46.

52 P. Taramarcaz et al., 'Ragweed (*Ambrosia*) Progression and Its Health Risks: Will Switzerland Resist This Invasion?', *Swiss Medical Weekly*, CXXXV (2005), pp. 538–48.

53 L. Kiss, 'Why Is Biocontrol of Common Ragweed, the Most Allergenic Weed in Eastern Europe, Still Only a Hope?', in *Biological Control: A Global Perspective*, ed., C. Vincent et al. (Wallingford, 2007), pp. 80–92.

54 F. C. Wilmott and G. W. Robertson, '*Senecio* Disease, or Cirrhosis of the Liver Due to *Senecio* Poisoning', *The Lancet*, CXCVI (1920), pp. 848–9.

55 Frohne and Pfänder, *Poisonous Plants*; S. Stockman, 'Poisoning of Cattle with British Ragwort', *Journal of Comparative Pathology and Theraputics*, XXX (1917), pp. 131–4.

56 M. Y. Altaee and M. H. Mahmood, 'An Outbreak of Veno-occlusive Disease of the Liver in Northern Iraq', *Eastern Mediterranean Health Journal*, IV

(1998), pp. 142–8; R. J. Huxtable, 'Herbal Teas and Toxins: Novel Aspects of Pyrrolizidine Poisoning in the United States', *Perspectives in Biology and Medicine*, XXIV (1980), pp. 1–14; E. Röder, 'Medical Plants in Europe Containing Pyrrolizidine Alkaloids', *Pharmazie*, L (1995), pp. 83–98; E. Röder, 'Medicinal Plants in China Containing Pyrrolizidine Alkaloids', *Pharmazie*, LV (2000), pp. 711–26; Frohne and Pfänder, *Poisonous Plants*; H. J. de Boer et al., 'DNA Barcoding Reveals Limited Accuracy of Identifications Based on Folk Taxonomy', *PLOS One*, IX (2014), p. e84291.

57 J. E. Peterson and C.C.J. Culvenor, 'Hepatotoxic Pyrrolizidine Alkaloids', in *Handbook of Natural Toxins, Volume I: Plant and Fungal Toxins*, ed. R. F. Keeler and A. T. Tu (New York, 1983), pp. 637–71.

58 R. Fisher, *The English Names of our Commonest Wild Flowers* (Arbroath, 1932).

59 M. Grieve, *A Modern Herbal* (London, 1979).

60 R. Page, 'Nothing to Lose but Our Ragwort', *Daily Telegraph Weekend*, 11 September 1993, p. III.

61 P. Ball, *Bright Earth: The Invention of Colour* (London, 2001).

62 H. Koster, *Travels in Brazil* (London, 1816), p. 495.

63 M. A. Chapman et al., 'Population Genetic Analysis of Safflower (*Carthamus tinctorius*; Asteraceae) Reveals a Near Eastern Origin and Five Centers of Diversity', *American Journal of Botany*, XCVII (2010), pp. 831–40; M. A. Chapman and J. M. Burke, 'DNA Sequence Diversity and the Origin of Cultivated Safflower (*Carthamus tinctorius* L.; Asteraceae)', *BMC Plant Biology*, VII (2007), p. 60.

64 C. Clementi et al., '*Carthamus tinctorius* L.: A Photophysical Study of the Main Coloured Species for Artwork Diagnostic Purposes', *Dyes and Pigments*, CIII (2014), pp. 127–37.

65 E. A. Weiss, *Castor, Sesame and Safflower* (New York, 1971).

66 L. Dajue and H.-H. Mündel, *Safflower: Carthamus tinctorius L.* (Rome, 1996).

67 D. Zohary et al., *Domestication of Plants in the Old World* (Oxford, 2013).

68 R. Nakamura et al., 'Scientific Evidence by Fluorescence Spectrometry for Safflower Red on Ancient Japanese Textiles Stored in the Shosoin Treasure House Repository', *Studies in Conservation*, LIX (2014), pp. 367–76.

69 E. S. Levine and W. Green, 'The Cosmetic Mystique of Old Japan', *Impressions*, IV (1980), pp. [1–5]; E. Strange, *Tools and Materials Illustrating the Japanese Method of Colour-printing: A Descriptive Catalogue of a Collection Exhibited in the Museum* (London, 1913).

70 E. F. Armstrong, 'Pigments of Other Days – I', *Journal of the Royal Society of Arts*, LXXXVII (1939), pp. 295–8.

5 Feeding

1 National Research Council, *Lost Crops of the Incas: Little Known Plants from the Andes with Promise for Worldwide Cultivation* (Washington, DC, 1989).

2 A. McFarlane, *The God Min to the End of the Old Kingdom* (Sydney, 1995).

3 D. Zohary et al., *Domestication of Plants in the Old World* (Oxford, 2013), p. 157.

4 U. P. Hedrick, *Sturtevant's Notes on Edible Plants* (Albany, NY, 1919).

5 A. Cowley, *The Third Part of the Works of Mr Abraham Cowley, Being His Six Books of Plants* (London, 1689), p. 16.

6 John Evelyn, *Acetaria: A Discourse of Sallets* (London, 1699), p. 32.

7 Martial, 'To Phoebus', in D. R. Shackleton Bailey, *Martial: Epigrams, Volume I, Spectacles, Books 1–5* (Cambridge, MA, 1993), Book 3, p. 89.

8 Martial, 'Lettuce', in D. R. Shackleton Bailey, *Martial: Epigrams, Volume III, Books 11–14* (Cambridge, MA, 1993), Book 13, p. 14.

9 P. A. Clement, *Plutarch: Moralia, Volume VIII, Table-talk, Books 1–6* (Cambridge, MA, 1969), Book 4.10, p. 672.

10 J. Parkinson, *Paradisi in Sole* (London, 1629), p. 499.

11 J. Gerard, *The Herball, or, Generall Historie of Plantes* (London, 1633), pp. 308, 310.

12 F. Harris, 'The Manuscripts of John Evelyn's "Elysium Britannicum"', *Garden History*, XXV (1997), pp. 131–7.

13 Evelyn, *Acetaria*, p. 31.

14 Parkinson, *Paradisi in Sole*, p. 498.

15 Evelyn, *Acetaria*, p. 34.

16 Gerard, *The Herball*, p. 307.

17 Evelyn, *Acetaria*, p. 33.

18 D. Zohary, 'The Wild Genetic Resources of Lettuce (*Lactuca sativa* L.)', *Euphytica*, LIII (1991), pp. 31–5; W.J.M. Koopman et al., 'Phylogenetic Relationships among *Lactuca* (Asteraceae) Species and Related Genera Based on ITS-1 DNA Sequences', *American Journal of Botany*, LXXXV (1998), pp. 1517–30; W.J.M. Koopman et al., 'Species Relationships in *Lactuca* s.l. (Lactuceae, Asteraceae) Inferred From AFLP Fingerprints', *American Journal of Botany*, LXXXVIII (2001), pp. 1881–7.

19 I. M. de Vries, 'Origin and Domestication of *Lactuca sativa* L.', *Genetic Resources and Crop Evolution*, XLIV (1997), pp. 165–74.

20 J. G. Vaughan and C. A. Geissler, *The New Oxford Book of Food Plants* (Oxford, 1999).

21 Food and Agriculture Organization of the United Nations, FAOSTAT 2014, www.fao.org (accessed 1 April 2015).

22 C. A. Stace and M. J. Crawley, *Alien Plants* (London, 2015).

23 T. Venner, *Via Recta ad Vitam Longam* (London, 1620), p. 134.

24 Parkinson, *Paradisi in Sole*, p. 516.

25 Gerard, *The Herball*, p. 752.

26 Ibid.

27 Ibid., p. 754.

28 Ibid.

29 D. E. Moerman, *Native American Ethnobotany* (Portland, OR, 1998), p. 259; S. de Champlain, *Les Voyages de la Nouvelle-France Occidentale* (Paris, 1632).

30 J. H. Trumbull and A. Gray, 'Notes on the History of *Helianthus tuberosus*, the So-called Jerusalem Artichoke', *Botanical Gazette*, II (1877), pp. 347–52;

S. Knapp, 'Why Is a Raven Like a Writing Desk? Origins of the Sunflower That Is Neither an Artichoke Nor from Jerusalem', *New Phytologist*, CCI (2014), pp. 710–11.

31 Trumbull, 'Notes on the History of *Helianthus tuberosus*', p. 348;
E. E. Schilling et al., 'Phylogenetic Relationships in *Helianthus* (Asteraceae) Based on Nuclear Ribosomal DNA Internal Transcribed Spacer Region Sequence Data', *Systematic Botany*, XXIII (1998), pp. 177–87; R. E. Timme et al., 'High-resolution Phylogeny for *Helianthus* (Asteraceae) Using the 18s–26s Ribosomal DNA External Transcribed Spacer', *American Journal of Botany*, XCIV (2007), pp. 1837–52.

32 D. G. Bock et al., 'Genome Skimming Reveals the Origin of the Jerusalem Artichoke Tuber Crop Species: Neither from Jerusalem nor an Artichoke', *New Phytologist*, CCI (2014), pp. 1021–30.

33 Gerard, *The Herball*, p. 754.

34 Parkinson, *Paradisi in Sole*, p. 518.

35 Knapp, 'Why Is a Raven Like a Writing Desk?', pp. 710–11.

36 C. H. Zhao, 'Inulin in the Application of Bio-energy', *Advanced Materials Research*, CCCXLIII–CCCXLIV (2011), pp. 556–9.

37 Hedrick, *Sturtevant's Notes on Edible Plants*.

38 J. Lightfoot, *Flora Scotica. Vol. 1* (London, 1777), p. 459.

39 G. Sonnante et al., 'On the Origin of Artichoke and Cardoon from the *Cynara* Gene Pool as Revealed by rDNA Sequence Variation', *Genetic Resources and Crop Evolution*, LIV (2007), pp. 483–95.

40 A. Wiklund, 'The Genus *Cynara* L. (Asteraceae-Cardueae)', *Botanical Journal of the Linnean Society*, CIX (1992), pp. 75–123.

41 Sonnante, 'On the Origin of Artichoke and Cardoon'.

42 Hedrick, *Sturtevant's Notes on Edible Plants*.

43 G. Sonnante 'The Domestication of Artichoke and Cardoon: From Roman Times to the Genomic Age', *Annals of Botany*, C (2007), pp. 1095–1100.

44 C. Darwin, *The Origin of Species and the Voyage of the Beagle* (London, 2003), p. 161.

45 Gerarde, *The Herball*, p. 651.

46 S. Pepys, *The Illustrated Pepys: Extracts from the Diary* (Berkeley, CA, 1978), p. 105.

47 W. Gelleroy, *The London Cook, or the Whole Art of Cookery Made Easy and Familiar* (London, 1762), pp. 214–16.

48 W. Law, *The History of Coffee, Including a Chapter on Chicory* (London, 1850), p. 36.

49 P. L. Simmonds, *Coffee as It Is, and as It Ought to Be* (London, 1850), p. 15.

50 Law, *History of Coffee*, p. 36.

51 P. L. Simmonds, *Coffee and Chicory: Their Culture, Chemical Composition, Preparation for Market, and Consumption; With Simple Tests for Detecting Adulteration, and Practical Hints for the Producer and Consumer* (London, 1864).

52 F. Accum, *A Treatise on Adulteration of Food* (London, 1820).

53 Quoted in Law, *History of Coffee*, p. 46.

54 Simmonds, *Coffee and Chicory*, p. 292; Anon., *Report of the Proceedings on the Part of the Coffee Interest in Opposition to the Chicory Fraud: With Objections to the Treasury Minute Legalising the Sale of Mixtures of Chicory and Coffee* (London, 1853); Law, *History of Coffee*, pp. 38–43.

55 Simmonds, *Coffee as It Is* (London, 1850).

56 Law, *History of Coffee*, p. 46.

57 W. D. Seymour, *How to Employ Capital in Western Ireland: Answers to a Few Practical Questions upon the Manufacture of Beet-Sugar, Flax and Chicory* (London, 1851).

58 Proverbs 5:4.

59 Committee on Herbal Medicinal Products, *Assessment Report on Artemisia absinthium L., Herba* (London, 2009). Bitterness value of 10,000, with the assumption that an Olympic-sized swimming pool contains 2,500,000 litres (4,400,000 pints) of water and 'a handful' weighs about 250 g (9 oz).

60 W. N. Arnold, 'Absinthe', *Scientific American*, CCLX (1989, June), pp. 112–17.

61 B. Conrad, *Absinthe: History in a Bottle* (San Francisco, CA, 1988).

62 W. A. Arnold, 'Vincent van Gogh and the Thujone Connection', *Journal of the American Medical Association*, CCLX (1988), pp. 3042–4; D. Blumer, 'The Illness of Vincent van Gogh', *American Journal of Psychiatry*, CLIX (2002), pp. 519–26.

63 D. W. Lachenmeier et al., 'Absinthe – A Review', *Critical Reviews in Food Science and Nutrition*, XLVI (2006), pp. 365–77.

6 Profiting

1 M. Mazoyer and L. Roudart, *A History of World Agriculture from the Neolithic Age to the Current Crisis* (London, 2006).

2 P. Gerland et al., 'World Population Stabilization Unlikely This Century', *Science*, CCCXLVI (2014), pp. 234–7.

3 Food and Agriculture Organization of the United Nations, FAOSTAT 2014, www.fao.org (accessed 30 September 2015).

4 B. D. Smith, 'The Domestication of *Helianthus annuus* L. (Sunflower)', *Vegetation History and Archaeobotany*, XXIII (2014), pp. 57–74; B. K. Blackman et al., 'Sunflower Domestication Alleles Support Single Domestication Center in Eastern North America', *Proceedings of the National Academy of Sciences USA*, CVIII (2011), pp. 14360–65.

5 D. L. Lentz et al., 'Sunflower (*Helianthus annuus* L.) as a Pre-Columbian Domesticate in Mexico', *Proceedings of the National Academy of Sciences USA*, CV (2008), pp. 6232–7; C. B. Heiser, 'Sunflowers among Aztecs?', *International Journal of Plant Sciences*, CLXIX (2008), p. 980; D. L. Lentz, 'Reply to Heiser', *International Journal of Plant Sciences*, CLXIX (2008), p. 980; C. B. Heiser, 'The Sunflower (*Helianthus annuus*) in Mexico: Further Evidence for a North American Domestication', *Genetic Resources and Crop Evolution*, LV (2008), pp. 9–13.

6 J. Diamond, *Guns, Germs and Steel* (New York, 2003).

7 D. E. Moerman, *Native American Ethnobotany* (Portland, OR, 1998), pp. 257–8; C. B. Heiser, 'The Sunflower Among the North American Indians', *Proceedings of the American Philosophical Society*, XCV (1951), pp. 432–48.

8 J. Parkinson, *Paradisi in Sole* (London, 1629), pp. 295–6.

9 G. List, 'Market Report: Sunflower Seed and Oil', *Lipid Technology*, XXVII (2015), p. 24.

10 Food and Agriculture Organization of the United Nations, FAOSTAT 2014.

11 Russia is taken to mean the Russian Federation and those states that border the Russian Federation that were part of the former Soviet Union. At appropriate historical points, Russia is also taken to refer to the Soviet Union.

12 J. R. Lofgren, 'Sunflower for Confectionery Food, Bird Food, and Pet Food', in *Sunflower Production and Technology*, ed. A. A. Schneiter (Madison, WI, 1997), pp. 747–64.

13 Food and Agriculture Organization of the United Nations, FAOSTAT 2014.

14 P. F. Knowles and A. Ashri, 'Safflower', in *Evolution of Crop Plants*, ed. J. Smartt and N. W. Simmonds (London, 1995), pp. 358–66; S. Hiremath and H. N. Murthy, 'Domestication of Niger (*Guizotia abyssinica*)', *Euphytica*, CCXXVIII (1988), pp. 225–8; Dempewolf et al., 'Patterns of Domestication in the Ethiopian Oil-seed Crop Noug (*Guizotia abyssinica*)', *Evolutionary Applications*, VIII (2015), pp. 464–75.

15 E. Marinova and S. Riehl, '*Carthamus* Species in the Ancient Near East and South-southeastern Europe: Archaeobotanical Evidence for Their Distribution and Use as a Source of Oil', *Vegetation History and Archaeobotany*, XVIII (2009), pp. 341–9; S. J. Boardman, 'The Agricultural Foundation of the Aksumite Empire, Ethiopia', in *The Exploitation of Plant Resources in Ancient Africa*, ed. M. van der Veen (New York, 1999), pp. 137–47.

16 D. Russo et al., 'State of the Art of Biofuels from Pure Plant Oil', *Renewable and Sustainable Energy Reviews*, XVI (2012), pp. 4056–70.

17 C. B. Heiser, 'The Origin and Development of the Cultivated Sunflower', *American Biology Teacher*, XVII (1955), pp. 161–7; J. M. Fernández-Martínez et al., 'Sunflower', in *Oil Crops: Handbook of Plant Breeding IV*, ed. J. Vollmann and I. Rajcan (Dordrecht, 2009), pp. 155–232.

18 E. D. Putt, 'Early History of Sunflower', in *Sunflower Technology and Production*, ed. Schneiter.

19 Fernández-Martínez, 'Sunflower'.

20 D. E. Alexander, 'The "Lysenko" Method of Increasing Oil Content of the Sunflower', *Crop Science*, 11 (1963), pp. 279–80; S. V. Gontcharov and N. D. Beresneva, 'Confectionery Hybrid Sunflower Breeding in Russia', *Journal of Agricultural Science and Technology*, 1 (2011), pp. 919–24.

21 C. Watkins, 'Operation Oilseed', *Sunflower Magazine*, www.sunflowernsa.com (accessed 13 July 2015).

22 Fernández-Martínez, 'Sunflower'.

23 G. P. Nabhan, *Where Our Food Comes From: Retracing Nikolay Vavilov's Quest to End Famine* (Washington, DC, 2008); J. R. Harlan, *Crops and Man* (Madison, WI, 1992).

24 V. A. Gavrilova et al., 'Sunflower Genetic Collection at the Vavilov Institute of Plant Industry', *Helia*, XXXVII (2014), pp. 1–16.

25 P. Thomson, *Seeds, Sex and Civilization* (London, 2010).

26 W. Steffen et al., 'The Anthropocene: Conceptual and Historical Perspectives', *Philosophical Transactions of the Royal Society A*, CCCLXIX (2011), pp. 842–67.

27 J. Rockström et al., 'A Safe Operating Space for Humanity', *Nature*, CDLXI (2009), pp. 472–5.

28 W. Steffen et al., 'Planetary Boundaries: Guiding Human Development on a Changing Planet', *Science*, CCCXLVII (2015).

7 Influencing

1 V. van den Eynden, 'Plants as Symbols in Scotland', in *Ethnobotany in the New Europe: People, Health and Wild Plant Resources*, ed. M. Pardo-de-Santayana et al. (Oxford, 2013), pp. 239–45.

2 R. Mabey, *Flora Britannica: The Definitive New Guide to Wild Flowers, Plants and Trees* (London, 1996); W. Milliken and S. Bridgewater, *Flora Celtica: Plants and People in Scotland* (Edinburgh, 2013).

3 R. Kandeler and W. R. Ullrich, 'Symbolism of Plants: Examples from European-Mediterranean Culture Presented with Biology and History of Art. September: Cornflower', *Journal of Experimental Botany*, LX (2009), pp. 3297–9.

4 J. Goody, *The Culture of Flowers* (Cambridge, 1993).

5 A. Donnelly, 'Sunflower Mementoes for the Families of MH17 Victims', BBC News, 16 July 2015, http://news.bbc.com.

6 N. Guéguen, '"Say It with Flowers": The Effect of Flowers on Mating Attractiveness and Behavior', *Social Influence*, VI (2011), pp. 105–12; J. Haviland-Jones et al., 'An Environmental Approach to Positive Emotion: Flowers', *Journal of Evolutionary Psychology*, III (2005), pp. 104–32.

7 A. G. Morton, *History of Botanical Science: An Account of the Development of Botany from Ancient Times to the Present Day* (London, 1981).

8 J. Prest, *The Garden of Eden: The Botanic Garden and the Re-creation of Paradise* (London, 1981).

9 Goody, *The Culture of Flowers*.

10 F. Shoberl, *The Language of Flowers with Illustrative Poetry* (London, 1835), pp. 6–7.

11 S. W. Partridge, *Voices from the Garden; Or, the Christian Language of Flowers* (London, 1849), Preface.

12 Ibid.

13 C. H. Waterman, *Flora's Lexicon: An Interpretation of the Language and Sentiment of Flowers: With an Outline of Botany, and a Poetical Introduction* (Boston, MA, 1852); H. G. Adams, *The Language and Poetry of Flowers* (New York, 1859).

14 Waterman, *Flora's Lexicon*; Dumont, *The Language of Flowers* (Philadelphia, PA, 1852); Adams, *Language and Poetry of Flowers*; Partridge, *Voices from the Garden*.

15 Adams, *Language and Poetry of Flowers*.

16 Waterman, *Flora's Lexicon*; Dumont, *Language of Flowers*; Adams, *Language and Poetry of Flowers*; Partridge, *Voices from the Garden*.

17 Goody, *Culture of Flowers*.

18 B. Berlin, *Ethnobiological Classification: Principles of Categorization of Plants and Animals in Traditional Societies* (Princeton, NJ, 1992).

19 G. Grigson, *A Dictionary of English Plant Names (And Some Products of Plants)* (London, 1973), p. 94.

20 R. Fisher, *The English Names of our Commonest Wild Flowers* (Arbroath, 1932).

21 K. Thomas, *Man and the Natural World: Changing Attitudes in England, 1500–1800* (London, 1983), pp. 81–7.

22 Anon., 'Editor to Correspondent N.F.', *Gardeners' Chronicle*, I (1841), p. 737.

23 C. Linnaeus, *Critica Botanica* (Leiden, 1737), pp. 79–81.

24 W. Blunt, *Linnaeus: The Compleat Naturalist* (London, 2004), pp. 121–2.

25 R. Bernstein, 'Vienna Journal; The Hills Are Alive with the Sound of Remembrance', *New York Times*, 24 March 2005.

26 T. Scheidegger, *Mythos Edelweiss: Zur Kulturgeschichte eines Alpinen Symbols* (Geneva, 2008), www.isek.uzh.ch.

27 Whether one species with two subspecies, or two species, should be recognized is a point of taxonomic debate. Genetic data supports the recognition of two species. C. Blöch et al., 'Molecular Phylogeny of the Edelweiss (*Leontopodium*, Asteraceae–Gnaphalieae)', *Edinburgh Journal of Botany*, LXVII (2010), pp. 235–64; S. Safer et al., 'Phylogenetic Relationships in the Genus *Leontopodium* (Asteraceae: Gnaphalieae) Based on AFLP Data', *Botanical Journal of the Linnean Society*, CLXV (2011), pp. 364–77.

28 M. Ischer et al., 'A Better Understanding of the Ecological Conditions for *Leontopodium alpinum* Cassini in the Swiss Alps', *Folia Geobotanica*, XLIX (2014), pp. 541–58.

29 C. Boner, 'Chamois Hunting in the Mountains of Bavaria', *New Monthly Magazine*, XCVIII (1853), p. 166.

30 B. Auerbach, *Edelweiss: A Story* (Boston, MA, 1869), p. 77.

31 Y. Ballu, *Die Alpen auf Plakaten* (Bern, 1987).

32 G. Flemwell, *Alpine Flowers and Gardens* (London, 1910), p. 90.

33 Henry Correvon in G. Flemwell, *The Flower-fields of Alpine Switzerland: An Appreciation and a Plea* (London, 1911), Preface.

34 W. S. Walsh, *Handy-book of Literary Curiosities* (Philadelphia, PA, 1909), p. 268.

35 M. Twain, *A Tramp Abroad* (London, 1880), p. 216.

36 Flemwell, *Flower-fields of Alpine Switzerland*, p. 36.

37 P. Martin, *The Chrysanthemum Throne: A History of the Emperors of Japan* (Honolulu, HI, 1997).

38 Anon., 'Dahlia: National Flower of Mexico', http://en.presidencia.gob.mx (accessed 1 September 2016).

39 B. Bell, 'The Beautiful Flower with an Ugly Past', BBC News, 22 May 2016, http://news.bbc.com.

40 P. Biddiscombe, '"The Enemy of Our Enemy": A View of the Edelweiss Piraten from the British and American Archives', *Journal of Contemporary History*, xxx (1995), pp. 37–63.
41 J. Dormer, *A Collection of State Flowers* (London, 1734).
42 T. Rowlandson, *The Flower of the City* (London, 1809); C. Williams, *The Fadeing Flower: 'The Flower Fadeth and Its Place Shall Know It no More'* (London, 1809).
43 G. Cruikshank, *The Peddigree of Corporal Violet*, print published by Hannah Humphrey (London, 1815).
44 Scheidegger, *Mythos Edelweiss*, p. 26. For a personal view of alpine conservation in the early twentieth century, see Flemwell, *Alpine Flowers and Gardens*, pp. 133–5.
45 R. Mann, *Daisy Petals and Mushroom Clouds: LBJ, Barry Goldwater, and the Ad that Changed American Politics* (Baton Rouge, LA, 2011).

8 Civilizing

1 T. Hood, *The Poetical Works of Thomas Hood* (Boston, MA, 1869), p. 176.
2 T.H.B. Sofield et al., 'Historical Methodology and Sustainability: An 800-year-old Festival from China', *Journal of Sustainable Tourism*, I (1998), pp. 267–92; E. W. Clement, *The Japanese Floral Calendar* (Chicago, IL, 1905).
3 R. Mabey, *Flora Britannica: The Definitive New Guide to Wild Flowers, Plants and Trees* (London, 1996), pp. 354–5.
4 C. M. Skinner, *Myths and Legends of Flowers, Trees, Fruits, and Plants in All Ages and in All Climes* (Philadelphia, PA, 1911), pp. 83–4.
5 G. Grigson, *A Dictionary of English Plant Names (And Some Products of Plants)* (London, 1974), p. 42.
6 L. Parry, *William Morris Textiles* (London, 1983); O. Fairclough and E. Leary, *Textiles by William Morris and Morris and Co., 1861–1940* (London, 1981).
7 M. B. Freeman, *The Unicorn Tapestries* (New York, 1983).
8 W.H.S. Jones, *Pliny: Natural History, Books 24–27* (Cambridge, MA, 2001), Books 5, 4, 8.
9 G. Saunders, *Picturing Plants: An Analytical History of Botanical Illustration* (London, 1995), p. 7.
10 R. Addison, 'From My Own Apartment Window', *The Tatler*, 25 August 1710.
11 R. Hayden, *Mrs Delany: Her Life and Her Flowers* (London, 1980); M. Laird and A. Weisberg-Roberts, *Mrs Delany and Her Circle* (New Haven, CT, 2009); M. Peacock, *The Paper Garden: An Artist (Begins Her Life's Work) at 72* (New York, 2011).
12 B. F. Tobin, 'Virtuoso or Naturalist? Margaret Cavendish Bentinck, Duchess of Portland', in *Women and Curiosity in Early Modern England and France*, ed. L. Cottegnies et al. (Leiden, 2016), pp. 216–32.
13 G. Paston, *Mrs Delany (Mary Granville): A Memoir, 1700–1788* (London, 1900), pp. 229–30.

14 Ibid., pp. 230–31.
15 E. Darwin, *The Botanic Garden: A Poem, in Two Parts* (London, 1807),
    p. 53; Lady Llanover, *The Autobiography and Correspondence of Mary Glanville,
    Mrs Delany: With Interesting Reminiscences of King George the Third and Queen
    Charlotte* (London, 1862), p. 96.
16 Paston, *Mrs Delany*, p. 230.
17 J. Ruskin, *Proserpina: Studies of Wayside Flowers* (Orpington, 1879).
18 M. Collins, *Medieval Herbals: The Illustrative Traditions* (London, 2000).
19 P. D. Sorensen, 'The Dahlia: An Early History', *Arnoldia*, XXX (1970),
    pp. 121–38.
20 A. M. Coats, 'The Empress Joséphine', *Garden History*, V (1977),
    pp. 40–46; É. P. Ventenat, *Jardin de la Malmaison* (Paris, 1803).
21 G. L. Miller, *The Metamorphosis of Plants: Johann Wolfgang von Goethe*
    (Cambridge, MA, 2009).
22 A. G. Morton, *History of Botanical Science: An Account of the Development of
    Botany from Ancient Times to the Present Day* (London, 1981).
23 I. Stewart, *Life's Other Secret: The New Mathematics of the Living World*
    (Chichester, 1998), pp. 121–36.
24 J. A. Adam, *A Mathematical Nature Walk* (Princeton, NJ, 2009),
    pp. 31–42.
25 G. Markowsky, 'Misconceptions about the Golden Ratio', *College
    Mathematics Journal*, XXIII (1992), pp. 2–19.
26 H. Vogel, 'A Better Way to Construct a Sunflower Head', *Mathematical
    Biosciences*, XLIV (1979), pp. 179–89.
27 J. Swinton et al., 'Novel Fibonacci and Non-fibonacci Structure in the
    Sunflower: Results of a Citizen Science Experiment', *Royal Society Open
    Science*, III (2016), p. 160091.
28 Quoted in G. C. Druce, *The Flora of Northamptonshire* (Arbroath, 1930),
    p. civ.
29 G. Chaucer, 'Prologue to "The Legend of Good Women"', www.machias.
    edu (accessed 20 September 2017); S. Landsberg, *The Medieval Garden*
    (London, 2002).
30 D. Ewen, *American Popular Songs: From the Revolutionary War to the Present*
    (New York, 1966).
31 A. Reid, *Leningrad: Tragedy of a City under Siege, 1941–44* (London, 2011);
    G. P. Nabhan, *Where Our Food Comes From: Retracing Nikolay Vavilov's Quest to
    End Famine* (Washington, DC, 2009).

9 Cultivating

1 J. Paxton, *A Practical Treatise on the Cultivation of the Dahlia* (London, 1838),
   p. 4.
2 R. Duthie, *Florists' Flowers and Societies* (Princes Risborough, 1988).
3 Quoted in the entry for carnations by R. J. Thornton, *New Illustration of the
   Sexual System of Carolus von Linnaeus: And the Temple of Flora, or Garden of Nature*
   (London, 1807).

4   J. Cullen et al., *The European Garden Flora: A Manual for the Identification of Plants Cultivated in Europe, Both Out-of-doors and Under Glass. Volume v. Boraginaceae to Compositae* (Cambridge, 2011).

5   UN Trade Statistics, http://unstats.un.org (accessed 5 September 2016).

6   A. Hughes, 'Global Commodity Networks, Ethical Trade and Governmentality: Organizing Business Responsibility in the Kenyan Cut Flower Industry', *Transactions of the Institute of British Geographers*, XXVI (2001), pp. 390–406.

7   P. D. Sorensen, 'The Dahlia: An Early History', *Arnoldia*, XXX (1970), pp. 121–38.

8   J. Salter, *The Chrysanthemum; Its History and Culture* (London, 1865); Z. Wand et al., 'Existing Situation and Content of Ancient Chinese Manuals on Chrysanthemum', *Studies in the History of Natural Sciences*, January 2009.

9   S. Landsberg, *The Medieval Garden* (London, 2002).

10 R. Fortune, *Three Years' Wanderings in the Northern Provinces of China, Including a Visit to the Tea, Silk, and Cotton Countries: With an Account of the Agriculture and Horticulture of the Chinese, New Plants, etc.* (London, 1847), p. 154.

11 Guinness World Records, Tallest Sunflower, www.guinnessworldrecords. com (accessed 1 May 2016).

12 S. A. Harris, *Planting Paradise: Cultivating the Garden, 1501–1900* (Oxford, 2011).

13 R. Fortune, *Yedo and Peking: A Narrative of a Journey to the Capitals of Japan and China . . .* (London, 1863), p. 126.

14 N. B. Ward, *On the Growth of Plants in Closely Glazed Cases* (London, 1852).

15 Salter, *The Chrysanthemum*.

16 W. Curtis, '*Chrysanthemum indicum*. Indian Chrysanthemum', *Botanical Magazine*, IX (1795), t.327.

17 Salter, *The Chrysanthemum*.

18 Ibid., pp. 7–8.

19 Z. Shi et al., '*Chrysanthemum*', *Flora of China*, www.efloras.org (accessed 10 October 2016).

20 Fortune, *Three Years' Wanderings*.

21 Fortune, *Yedo and Peking*, p. 126.

22 H. V. Hansen, 'A Taxonomic Revision of the Genus *Gerbera* (Compositae, Mutisieae) Sections Gerbera, Parva, Piloselloides (in Africa), and Lasiopus', *Opera Botanica*, LXXVIII (1985); H. V. Hansen, 'A Story of the Cultivated *Gerbera*', *New Plantsman*, VI (1999), pp. 85–95.

23 J. D. Hooker, 'Gerbera jamesoni', *Curtis's Botanical Magazine*, LXV (1889), t.7087.

24 R. I. Lynch, '*Gerbera*, with a Coloured Plate of the New Hybrids', *Flora and Sylva*, III (1905), pp. 206–8; R. I. Lynch, 'Natural Variations of *Gerbera*', *Gardeners' Chronicle*, XL (1906), p. 314; R. I. Lynch, 'Hybrid Gerberas', *Gardeners' Chronicle*, XLV (1909), pp. 339–41.

25 K. R. Tourjee et al., 'Early Development of *Gerbera* as a Floricultural Crop', *HortTechnology*, IV (1994), pp. 34–40.

26 L. H. Brockway, *Science and Colonial Expansion: The Role of the British Royal Botanic Gardens* (New Haven, CT, 1979); C. Juma, *The Gene Hunters: Biotechnology and the Scramble for Seeds* (Princeton, NJ, 1989).

27 R. Fortune, *A Journey to the Tea Countries of China; Including Sung-lo and the Bohea Hills; With a Short Notice of the East India Company's Tea Plantations in the Himalaya Mountains* (London, 1852), pp. 123, 125.

28 Fortune, *Yedo and Peking*, p. 105.

29 G. N. Fick, 'Genetics of Floral Color and Morphology in Sunflowers', *Journal of Heredity*, LXVII (1976), pp. 227–30.

30 Anon., *Catalogus Plantarum Horti Medici Oxoniensis* (Oxford, 1648); P. Stephens and W. Browne, *Catalogus Horti Botanici Oxoniensis* (Oxford, 1658); J. Bobart, *Catalogus Herbarum ex horto Botanico Oxoniensi*, 1676 (MS Sherard 32, Sherardian Library of Plant Taxonomy, Bodleian Library, Oxford).

31 S. Ohno et al., 'Genetic Control of Anthrocyanin Synthesis in Dahlia (*Dahlia variabilis*)', in *Bulbous Plants Biotechnology*, ed. K. G. Ramawat and J. M. Mérillon (Boca Raton, FL, 2014), pp. 228–47.

32 M. A. Chapman et al., 'Genetic Analysis of Floral Symmetry in Van Gogh's Sunflowers Reveals Independent Recruitment of CYCLOIDEA Genes in the Asteraceae', *PLOS Genetics*, VIII (2012), p. e1002628.

33 R. D. Sargent, 'Floral Symmetry Affects Speciation Rates in Angiosperms', *Proceedings of the Royal Society of London, Series B Biological Sciences*, CCLXXI (2004), pp. 603–8.

34 S. Andersson, 'Pollinator and Nonpollinator Selection on Ray Morphology in *Leucanthemum vulgare* (Oxeye Daisy, Asteraceae)', *American Journal of Botany*, XCV (2008), pp. 1072–8; L. R. Nielsen et al., 'Selective Advantage of Ray Florets in *Scalesia affinis* and *S. pedunculata* (Asteraceae), Two Endemic Species from the Galapagos', *Evolutionary Ecology*, XVI (2002), pp. 139–53; T. F. Stuessy et al., 'Adaptive Significance of Ray Corollas in *Helianthus grosseserratus* (Compositae)', *American Midland Naturalist*, CXV (1986), pp. 191–7.

35 M. Williamson, *Biological Invasions* (London, 1996).

36 C. A. Stace and M. J. Crawley, *Alien Plants* (London, 2015).

37 Ibid., p. 100.

38 S. A. Harris, 'Introduction of Oxford Ragwort, *Senecio squalidus* L.(Asteraceae), to the United Kingdom', *Watsonia*, XXIV (2002), pp. 31–43.

39 J. E. Smith, *Flora Britannica. Vol. II* (London, 1800), p. 884; H. N. Ridley, *The Dispersal of Plants throughout the World* (Ashford, Kent, 1930), p. 629.

40 E. Allan and J. R. Pannell, 'Rapid Divergence in Physiological and Life-history Traits between Northern and Southern Populations of the British Introduced Neo-species, *Senecio squalidus*', *Oikos*, CXVIII (2009), pp. 1053–61.

41 G. C. Druce, *The Flora of Oxfordshire: A Topographical and Historical Account of the Flowering Plants and Ferns Found in the Country; With Biographical Notices of the Botanists Who Have Contributed to Oxfordshire Botany During the Last Four Centuries* (Oxford, 1927).

42 D. H. Kent, '*Senecio squalidus* L. in the British Isles. 3. East Anglia', *Transactions of the Norfolk and Norwich Naturalists' Society*, XVIII (1957), pp. 30–31.

43 W.H.O. Ernst, 'Invasion, Dispersal and Ecology of the South African Neophyte *Senecio inaequidens* in the Netherlands: From Wool Alien to Railway and Road Alien', *Acta botanica neerlandica*, XLVII (1998), pp. 131–51.

44 J. Amphlett and J. Rea, *The Botany of Worcestershire: An Account of the Flowering Plants, Ferns, Mosses, Hepatics, Lichens, Fungi and Freshwater Algae, Which Grow or Have Grown Spontaneously in the County of Worcester* (Birmingham, 1909); F. J. Hanbury and E. S. Marshall, *Flora of Kent* (London, 1899), p. 202; G. G[ulliver], '*Senecio squalidus*', *Hardwicke's Science-gossip for 1873*, 1874, p. 139.

45 The species are cardoon, chicory, endive, globe artichoke, Jerusalem artichoke, lettuce, niger, safflower, sunflower and yacón.

46 H. Dempewolf et al., 'Crop Domestication in the Compositae: A Family-wide Trait Assessment', *Genetic Resources and Crop Evolution*, LV (2008), pp. 1141–57.

Further Reading

Allen, D. E., and G. Hatfield, *Medicinal Plants in Folk Tradition: An Ethnobotany of Britain and Ireland* (Portland, OR, 2004)

Bell, A. D., and A. Bryan, *Plant Form: An Illustrated Guide to Flowering Plant Morphology* (Portland, OR, 2008)

Bonifacino, J. M., et al., 'A History of Research in Compositae: Early Beginnings to the Reading Meeting (1975)', in V. A. Funk et al., *Systematics, Evolution, and Biogeography of Compositae* (Vienna, 2009), pp. 3–38

Bremer, K., *Asteraceae: Cladistics and Classification* (Portland, OR, 1994)

Calabria, L. M., et al., 'Secondary Chemistry of Compositae', in Funk, *Systematics*, pp. 73–88

Conrad, B., *Absinthe: History in a Bottle* (San Francisco, CA, 1988)

Crosby, A. W., *The Columbian Exchange: Biological and Cultural Consequences of 1492* (Westport, CN, 2003)

Dajue, L., and H.-H. Mündel, *Safflower*: Carthamus tinctorius L. (Rome, 1996)

Dempewolf, H., et al., 'Crop Domestication in the Compositae: A Family-wide Trait Assessment', *Genetic Resources and Crop Evolution*, LV (2008), pp. 1141–57

Dunmire, W. M., *Gardens of New Spain: How Mediterranean Plants and Foods Changed America* (Austin, TX, 2004)

Fernández-Martínez, J. M., et al., 'Sunflower', in *Oil Crops: Handbook of Plant Breeding IV*, ed. J. Vollmann and I. Rajcan (Dordrecht, 2009), pp. 155–232

Frohne, D., and H. J. Pfänder, *Poisonous Plants: A Handbook for Doctors, Pharmacists, Toxicologists, Biologists and Veterinarians* (London, 2004)

Funk, V. A., et al., *Systematics, Evolution, and Biogeography of Compositae* (Vienna, 2009)

Goody, J., *The Culture of Flowers* (Cambridge, 1993)

Harlan, J. R., *Crops and Man* (Madison, WI, 1992)

Lüttge, U., *Physiological Ecology of Tropical Plants* (Berlin, 2008)

Mabey, R., *Flora Britannica: The Definitive New Guide to Wild Flowers, Plants and Trees* (London, 1996)

Mazoyer, M., and L. Roudart, *A History of World Agriculture from the Neolithic Age to the Current Crisis* (London, 2006)

Morton, A. G., *History of Botanical Science: An Account of the Development of Botany from Ancient Times to the Present Day* (London, 1981)

Nabhan, G. P., *Where Our Food Comes From: Retracing Nikolay Vavilov's Quest to End Famine* (Washington, DC, 2008)

Proctor, M., et al., *The Natural History of Pollination* (London, 1996)

Putt, E. D., 'Early History of Sunflower', in *Sunflower Technology and Production*, ed. A. A. Schneiter (Madison, WI, 1997)

Rieseberg, L. H., 'Hybrid Speciation in Wild Sunflowers', *Annals of the Missouri Botanical Garden*, XCIII (2006), pp. 34–48

Smith, B. D., 'The Domestication of *Helianthus annuus* L. (Sunflower)', *Vegetation History and Archaeobotany*, XXIII (2014), pp. 57–74

Sonnante, G., 'The Domestication of Artichoke and Cardoon: From Roman Times to the Genomic Age', *Annals of Botany*, C (2007), pp. 1095–100

Sorensen, P. D., 'The Dahlia: An Early History', *Arnoldia*, XXX (1970), pp. 121–38

Stace, C. A., et al., *Hybrid Flora of the British Isles* (Bristol, 2015)

—, and M. J. Crawley, *Alien Plants* (London, 2015)

Stewart, I., *Life's Other Secret: The New Mathematics of the Living World* (Chichester, 1998), pp. 121–36

Thomas, K., *Man and the Natural World: Changing Attitudes in England, 1500–1800* (London, 1983)

Vaughan, J. G., and C. A. Geissler, *The New Oxford Book of Food Plants* (Oxford, 1999)

Zohary, D., and M. Hopf, *Domestication of Plants in the Old World* (Oxford, 2000)

Associations and Websites

✿

THE AMERICAN DAHLIA SOCIETY
www.dahlia.org

ANGIOSPERM PHYLOGENY WEBSITE
www.mobot.org/MOBOT/Research/APweb

ASTERACEAE GENERA
www.theplantlist.org/browse/A/Compositae

BIODIVERSITY HERITAGE LIBRARY
www.biodiversitylibrary.org

THE BRITISH LEAFY SALAD ASSOCIATION
www.britishleafysalads.co.uk

FOOD AND AGRICULTURE ORGANIZATION OF THE UNITED NATIONS
www.fao.org

GLOBAL INVASIVE SPECIES DATABASE
www.iucngisd.org/gisd

INTERNATIONAL SUNFLOWER ASSOCIATION
http://isasunflower.org/home.html

NATIONAL CHRYSANTHEMUM SOCIETY
www.nationalchrysanthemumsociety.co.uk

NATIONAL CHRYSANTHEMUM SOCIETY, USA
www.mums.org

NATIONAL DAHLIA SOCIETY
www.dahlia-nds.co.uk

NATIONAL SUNFLOWER ASSOCIATION
www.sunflowernsa.com

Acknowledgements

✿

I would like to thank the Department of Plant Sciences and the Bodleian Library Services for access to the archival resources of Oxford University Herbaria and the Sherardian Library of Plant Taxonomy.

Photo Acknowledgements

The author and the publishers wish to express their thanks to the below sources of illustrative material and/or permission to reproduce it.

The J. Paul Getty Museum, Los Angeles: pp. 11, 54, 160, 169, 175, 185; S. A. Harris: pp. 6, 10, 12, 17, 28, 33, 35, 38, 40, 45, 51, 56, 57, 60, 70–71, 73, 75, 78, 86, 87, 88, 91, 93, 95, 96, 104, 116, 119, 130, 138, 140, 142, 145, 147, 156, 171, 172, 176, 178–9, 180, 182, 188, 190, 199; The Metropolitan Museum of Art, New York: pp. 15, 83, 105, 111, 159, 163, 165, 187; Private Collection: pp. 14, 18, 19, 20, 23, 31, 34, 37, 39, 46, 48, 55, 63, 65, 66, 67, 72, 92, 101, 106, 109, 112, 115, 117, 127, 148, 149, 152, 154, 161, 185, 192, 195, 196; REX Shutterstock: p. 135 (Tony Kyriacou); Sherardian Library of Plant Taxonomy, Oxford University Herbaria: pp. 9, 24, 27, 44, 77, 153, 168.

Index

Page numbers in *italics* refer to illustrations